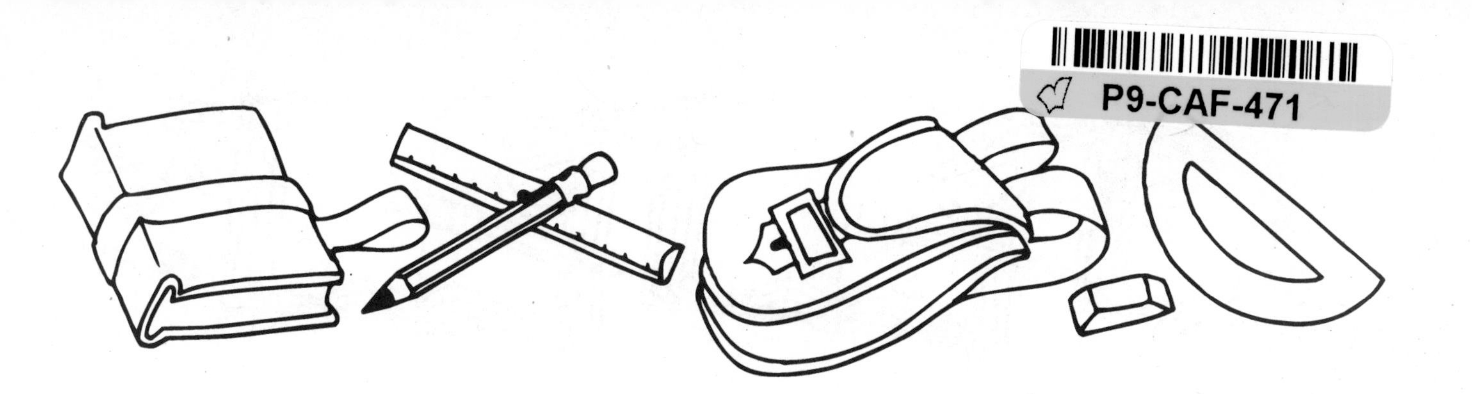

Quick and Easy Teacher Tips

Good Apple

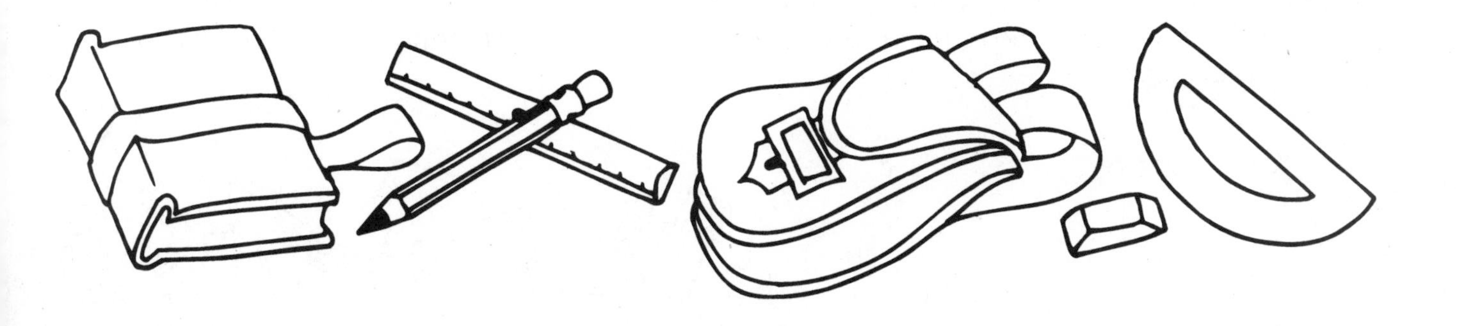

Editor: Donna Borst

Interior Illustration: Vanessa Filkins

Cover Design: Signature Design Group, Inc.

GOOD APPLE
A Division of Frank Schaffer Publications, Inc.
23740 Hawthorne Blvd.
Torrance, CA 90505

GA1650 ISBN 1-56417-981-8

2 3 4 5 6 7 8 9

Table of Contents

To The Teacher

In this book, you will find a compilation of the very best teaching tips from over 120 issues of ***The Good Apple Newspaper.*** Good Apple has long been known for our quick, easy-to-use, teacher-tested ideas. Now that we've been around for 25 years, we have decided it is time to dust off the shelves and put together this book to share some of these ideas with you again. If you're a new teacher, this book will be a resource you will use time and time again throughout your teaching career. If you're a seasoned veteran, you will be thrilled to have so many good ideas right at your fingertips in one handy resource.

We have ideas for every subject area including math, language arts, science, and social studies. We have tips for getting ready for back-to-school, and we have included some great ideas for bulletin boards and learning centers. There are creative, quick activities for your arts-and-crafts program and a huge selection of seasonal teacher tips. Then to top it off, we've added a number of tips in a general category—ideas that are just too good to leave out but don't quite fit into any specific subject area.

Once again, Good Apple has come through with another top-notch teacher resource that will be invaluable to your classroom. ***Quick and Easy Teacher Tips*** will provide you with enough new ideas for many years to come. This is one resource you'll want to keep right on your desk so that it is always there when you need a new, quick idea.

If you have ideas that you would like to share with other teachers through ***The Good Apple Newspaper,*** we would love to hear from you. You may submit your ideas to ***The Good Apple Newspaper***, 3427 Pheasant Run Drive, Wever, IA 52658. If you would like to subscribe to ***The Good Apple Newspaper,*** please call 1-800-264-9873.

Other books compiled from ***The Good Apple Newspaper:***
- ***The Best of The Good Apple Newspaper*** **(GA 1532)**
- ***The Best of The Good Apple Newspaper: Holidays & Seasons*** **(GA1651)**

Back-to-School

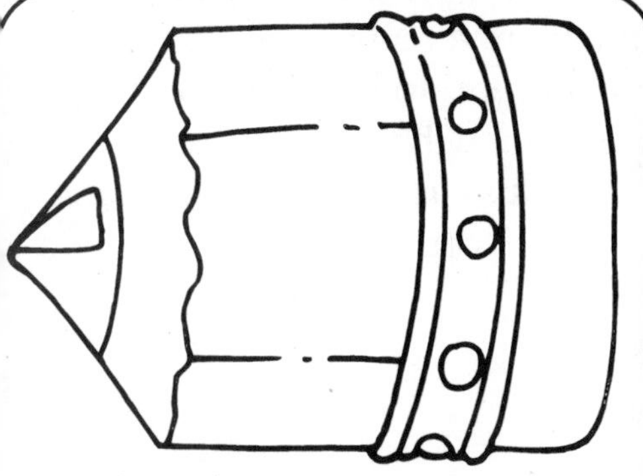

Ask each student to write and illustrate one sentence about: "Something I want to happen this year at school."

Then do your best to make those wishes come true during the year.

Dream up and stitch up a class crest or banner. Give each student a 6" (15 cm) square of burlap, a needle, and yarn. Have each student stitch a design that represents himself or herself. Sew all the squares together.

For your primary class, string up a time line with the names of the months taped or stapled on at 2' (.61 m) intervals. Clip each student's name and birthday in the proper place. Add other holidays and special events throughout the year. Use often for estimating time and so on.

Back-to-School

Trace around each student's head (or shine a light on them and trace the shadow) to make a profile silhouette. Give students their silhouettes, magazines, scissors, and glue, and ask them to "fill their heads" with pictures that show who they are. Display.

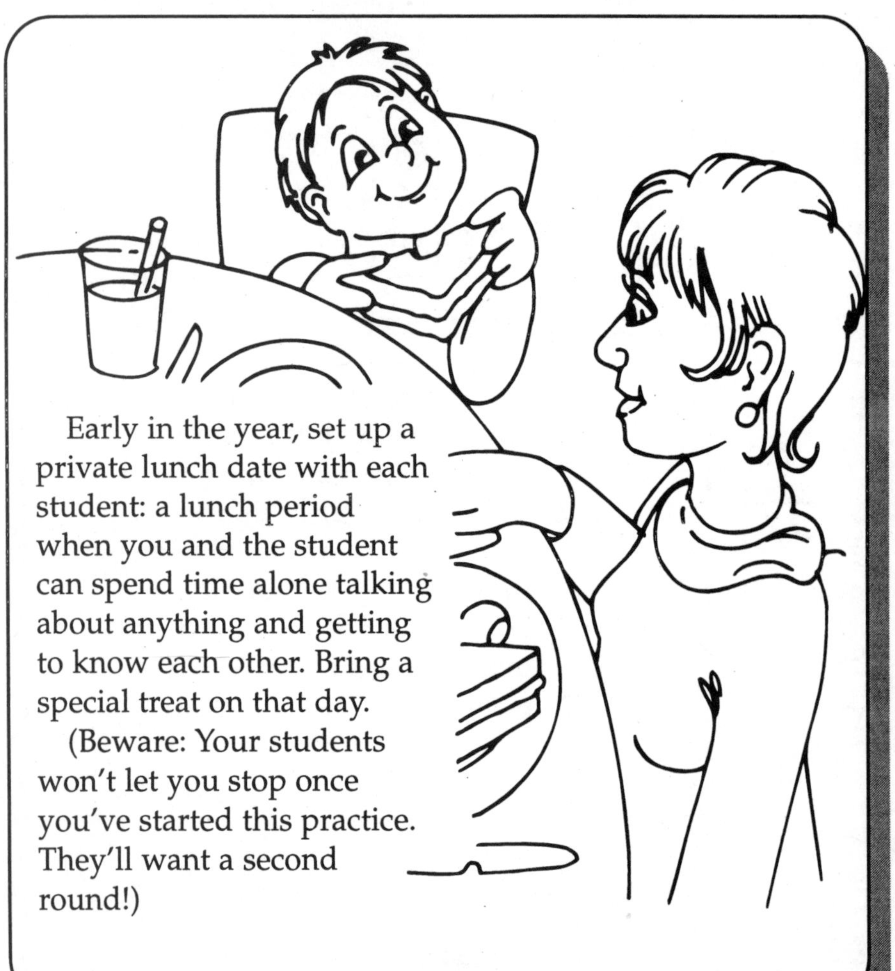

Early in the year, set up a private lunch date with each student: a lunch period when you and the student can spend time alone talking about anything and getting to know each other. Bring a special treat on that day.

(Beware: Your students won't let you stop once you've started this practice. They'll want a second round!)

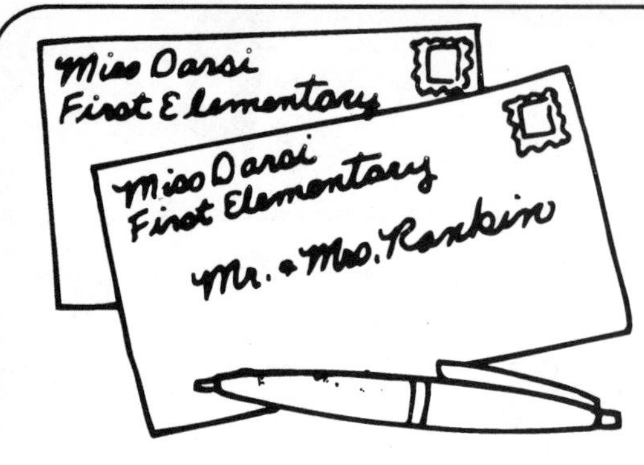

At the end of the first week of school, take time to write a short note to each student's parents, just to give them a few positive comments and to let them know you are in touch with their child as an individual. It will be a good start for effective communication.

Get to know your students by having them fill out an informal personal inventory. (Provided on page 8.)

Put up a measuring scale along the wall. (Do one in inches and one in centimeters.) Have students measure one another and mark their heights with arrows. Repeat the measurements midway through the year and at the end to compare heights. Or, students may enjoy graphing their growth every month.

Make a list of 10 promises to yourself: promises to accomplish new things you want to do. Read over your list often.

I Promise to . . .
1) Visit two new schools. 2) Call parents when good things are happening. 3) Take a walk during my lunch hour. 4) Read three professional books before Christmas. 5) Subscribe to a new magazine.
6) Throw away that old Africa unit and teach it in a new way. 7) Try a new idea once a week.
8) Go somewhere different on a field trip.

Choral reading is a good back-to-school activity because it is a fun, "together" effort. The sense of working together to produce a "choir" effect gives a good group feeling to any class. *Time for Poetry* by Arbuthant is a fine source of poems suitable for choral reading.

About Myself

My name is ______________________

Today I feel ______________________

Something special about me is ______________________

I'd rather ____________ than ______________________

I like teachers that ______________________

My favorite place to be is ______________________

Something that bothers me is ______________________

At our house we ______________________

Before I go to bed, I like to ______________________

When I'm alone ______________________

The most important person in the world is ______________________

I wish I could ______________________

Sometimes I like to ______________________

I think school should be a place where ______________________

I feel nervous when ______________________

I wish people wouldn't ______________________

It makes me angry when ______________________

Better than anything, I like ______________________

I really get angry when ______________________

I feel proud when ______________________

This year I hope ______________________

One thing I'd like to know about the teacher is ______________________

____

One thing I'd like the teacher to know about me is ______________________

____

Arts and Crafts

A Class Totem Pole

After discussing the history of totem poles of early America, make your own class totem pole to tell the story of each person in the class. Each student should choose an animal with which he or she has some characteristic in common. After drawing or tracing their animals, students can mount them on different-colored and different-shaped paper. Under their animals, have students explain the symbolic connection between themselves and the animals they chose. All animals are then mounted on top of each other vertically and displayed for all to read and enjoy.

Examples

1. The butterfly is a good symbol for me because I like to travel a lot.
2. The peacock is a good symbol for me because I like to show off or perform for others.
3. The lion is a good symbol for me because I'm a good leader.

Egg Carton Totem Poles

Supplies

- cardboard egg cartons
- markers or tempera paints
- glue
- scissors

Directions

1. Cut out the egg sections.
2. Before gluing them together, decide how you want each face to look. It will be easier to design and decorate the totem pole before the whole thing is glued together.
3. Glue the heads in place.
4. Cut up the lids of the egg carton to be used as a flat base or for wings, horns, hands, or ears.
5. Allow the totem pole to dry thoroughly.

Arts and Crafts

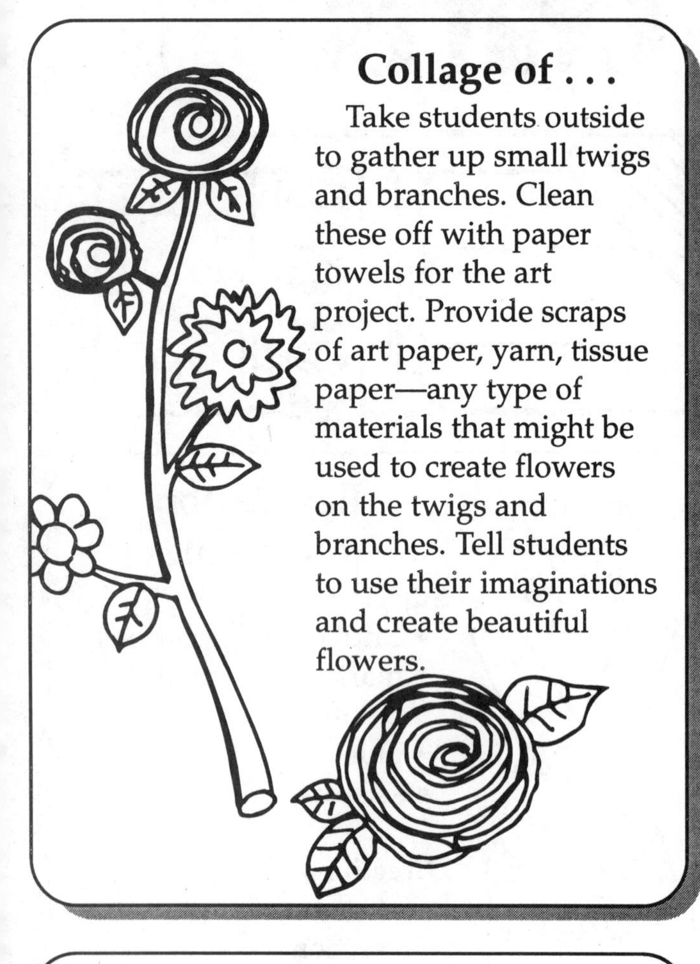

Collage of . . .

Take students outside to gather up small twigs and branches. Clean these off with paper towels for the art project. Provide scraps of art paper, yarn, tissue paper—any type of materials that might be used to create flowers on the twigs and branches. Tell students to use their imaginations and create beautiful flowers.

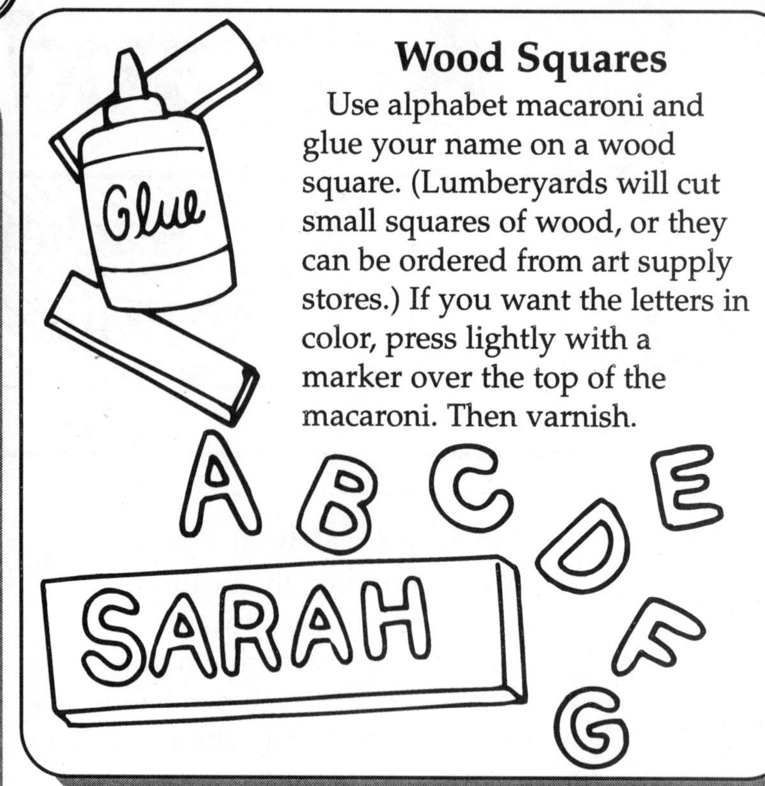

Wood Squares

Use alphabet macaroni and glue your name on a wood square. (Lumberyards will cut small squares of wood, or they can be ordered from art supply stores.) If you want the letters in color, press lightly with a marker over the top of the macaroni. Then varnish.

Stained-Glass Windows

First, make a frame from posterboard. Punch two holes at the top to thread yarn or ribbon through as a hanger. Give each student a sheet of waxed paper and white glue. Cut small squares of colorful tissue paper and glue these, overlapping them sightly, onto the waxed paper. After this dries completely, cut the sheet to fit behind the frame. Tape the "stained glass" in place. Hang this in a bright place for the sun to shine through.

Bookmark That Holds!

Materials

- wallpaper
- self-stick flat magnets
- laminating fill or contact paper

Directions

Cut wallpaper into strips (about 2" x 9" [5 x 23 cm]). Laminate the cut strips. Fold strips in half. Glue or stick two magnets at the inside bottom of the strip, one on each end.

The bookmark should be placed at the top or side of a page of a book so that the magnets hold together.

The bookmarks can be personalized any way you choose and make great gifts for the holidays.

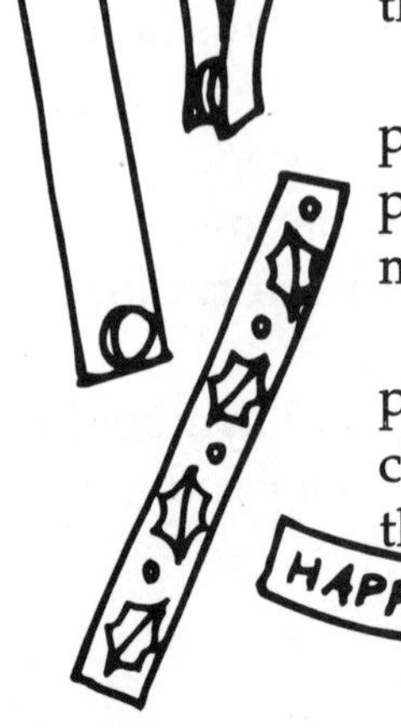

Apple Windows

Duplicate two apple patterns on red, green, or yellow construction paper for each student. Make sure each apple pattern has an inner line drawn around it approximately 3/4" from the outside edge. Have students cut out the center of each apple using the inner line as a guide. This will make an apple-shaped frame. Use the apple center as a pattern to cut two pieces of waxed paper, except cut waxed paper 1/4" (.6 cm) larger all the way around.

Have students shave crayon bits onto one of the pieces of waxed paper using a crayon sharpener, potato peeler, or a plastic knife; or you could do crayon shavings ahead of time and put each color into separate containers. Cover the shavings with the other piece of waxed paper. With a towel underneath and on top of the waxed paper, iron the papers together so the crayon shavings melt. Glue one apple frame to the waxed paper. Match up the second apple and glue to the other side so the waxed paper is sandwiched between the apple frames.

Hang apples from the ceiling on lights, or tape to walls or bulletin boards. Apple windows are displayed best when hung in a window where students can enjoy all the colors when the sun shines through the melted crayon.

Variation: Sandwich a piece of colored (red, green, or yellow) tissue paper or cellophane between two apple-shaped frames.

Making Bookmarks

Bookmarks are easy to make because students can make them any way they like. Almost any material can be used as long as it is thin: paper, cardboard, cloth, wrapping paper, ribbon, and so on. Any shape may be used for the bookmark, something roughly 2" x 5" (5 x 13 cm) is a good size. Paper and cardboard can be decorated with crayon or colored ink, cloth might be stitched or embroidered and sport a tassel, and a ribbon might have stickers pasted to it. The bookmarks can also be personalized with a name, initials, a slogan, or a verse.

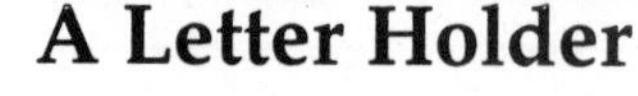

Orange-Peel Bird Feeder

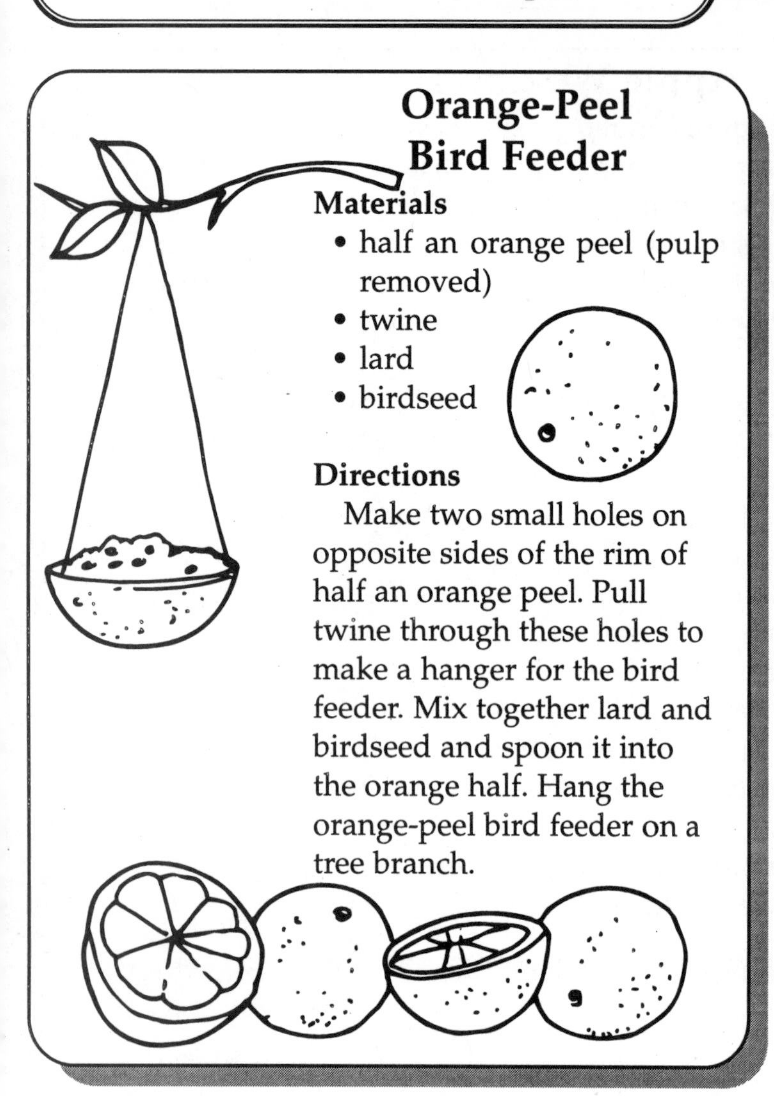

Materials

- half an orange peel (pulp removed)
- twine
- lard
- birdseed

Directions

Make two small holes on opposite sides of the rim of half an orange peel. Pull twine through these holes to make a hanger for the bird feeder. Mix together lard and birdseed and spoon it into the orange half. Hang the orange-peel bird feeder on a tree branch.

A Letter Holder

A common plastic dish detergent bottle can be made into an attractive letter holder. First cut off the top part of the detergent bottle and discard. Use a crayon to draw a cutting line on both sides of the remaining bottom half of the bottle as shown. Cut along these crayon lines on both sides of the bottle all the way down to the base.

The base structure of the letter holder is finished. Decorate the letter holder with acrylic paint or punch holes around the edges with a paper punch and weave yarn through the holes.

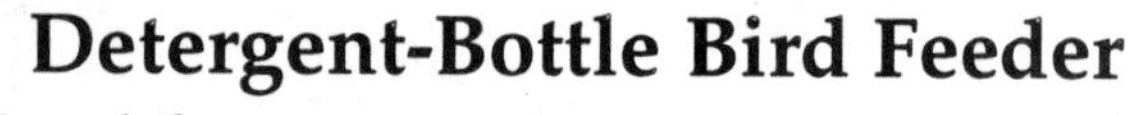

Detergent-Bottle Bird Feeder

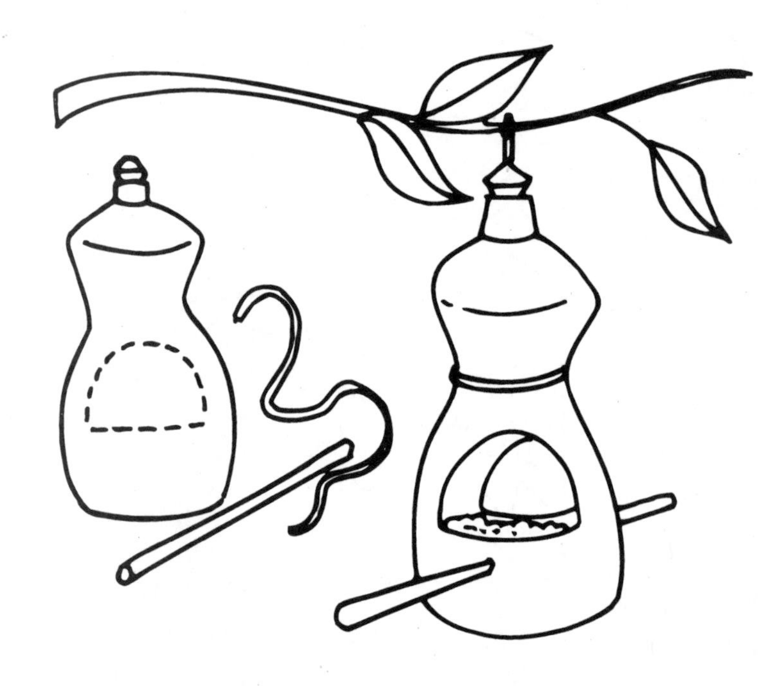

Materials

- plastic dish-detergent bottle
- small dowel
- twine
- birdseed

Directions

Wash and dry an empty plastic detergent bottle. Cut a hole on each side of the bottle that is big enough for a bird to put its head into. Make a small hole under the larger holes for a dowel that the birds can sit on. Tie twine around the top of the bottle to hang it on a tree branch. Fill the bottom of the bottle with birdseed.

Caterpillar

Create a colorful caterpillar from a sturdy paper towel tube. You'll also need scissors, white glue, a ruler, paint or colored paper, a length of heavy yarn, and a pipe cleaner cut in half.

Cut a section 1" to 1 1/4" wide along the length of the tube. This part can be thrown away. Cut the rest of the tube into rings about 3/4" wide. Make one ring a little wider for the head.

Paint or use colored paper to decorate the segments both inside and out. Put a face on the head segment. If you want to make eyes that stand up, cut out two small paper circles. Fold them in half, add pupils, and glue half of each circle to the head.

Lay all the segments upside down in a row about 3/4" part. Glue them to the yarn. Twist pipe cleaner antennae to the inside of the head.

Make Your Own Jewelry From Dough

If you've been searching for a way to make gifts stamped with originality, here is the answer. Making dough jewelry is fun and foolproof. Anyone can do it; here's how.

1. Mix flour and water until the resulting dough is very stiff. Then just keep kneading it until it is completely free of lumps. A drop of perfume added to it will lend a delightful fragrance.
2. Roll the dough into a slender cylinder about a 1/2" (1.25 cm) thick; then cut beads about 1/2" (1.25 cm) long. They can be left smooth or given an attractive appearance by using the prongs of a fork to make marks in each bead.
3. When the beads are stiff but not hard, string them together by pushing a needle and heavy thread through the center of each bead, allowing about 1/2" (1.25 cm) of thread to separate each bead. Then allow them to dry thoroughly.
4. After the beads are dried and hard, paint them with watercolors, or just dip them into paint. Then coat the beads with clear nail polish.
5. Now remove the original string and re-thread them with good mercerized thread. You can make a matching bracelet and earrings (use only one bead for each earring). Clip or screw earring backs can be purchased at any craft store; just glue them to the bead back. These make great gifts for students to give to parents and grandparents.

Arts and Crafts

Window Fish

Materials
- blown-out egg for each fish
- 20″ (50 cm) ribbon
- Easter-egg dye
- sequins (optional)
- white felt
- white glue

Directions
1. Dip the blown-out egg carefully into desired egg dye color. Let dry.
2. Using the patterns, cut two tails and lots of scales from white felt.
3. Give your fish two sequin eyes and a mouth. Glue the tail on smaller end of egg.
4. Glue the scales on the top part of the eggshell, straight edge against the shell. One sequin may be glued to the tip of each scale if you wish.
5. Glue ribbon to the top of fish and tie ends in a bow.

Hang your fish from the window. With a little breeze blowing in from the window, your fish looks like it is alive. It makes a lovely gift for someone in the hospital.

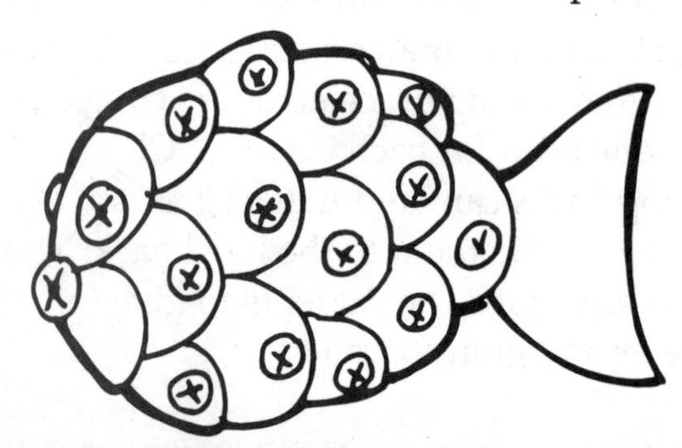

The Great Snowman Collage

Spark enthusiasm for wintertime by creating a snowman collage with the help of your class. Cut a big snowman shape out of white butcher paper. Display the snowman on a bulletin board. Ask your students to bring in pictures pertaining to winter. Create a seasonal collage by gluing these pictures on the snowman.

Make a Moonscape

Show students pictures of the moon's surface. Young students can form the valleys, hills, and craters with clay. Older students may enjoy working with papier-mâché.

Soak pieces of newspaper in a bowl of paste and cold water. Using a cardboard base, build hills and craters; then paint. Crumple sheets of soaked paper for the hills, then cover with smaller pieces. Use small pieces to form craters.

Construction-Paper Loop Art

Cut construction paper into various strips and staple the strips into loops, as in the diagrams below.

Bunny

Using one 8 1/2" x 11" (22 x 28 cm) sheet of pink construction paper, cut into one 5" x 11" (13 x 28 cm) piece (for the body) and one 3 1/2" x 11" (9 x 28 cm) piece (for the head).

Cut out two ears and two front paws from white paper. Attach the ears to the top of the head and the paws to the bottom of the head piece.

Draw on facial features with markers. Glue on a cotton ball for a tail. Staple the head and body together.

Chick

Cut two 1 1/2" strips of yellow construction paper. Cut out small orange strips for feet and a tail and attach as shown.

Cut out an orange paper beak and glue it to the head. Draw eyes with a black marker. Staple the head and body together.

Whimsical Windsocks

The popular windsock is seen flying everywhere across the country. Making paper windsocks is an exciting activity to enrich a unit on weather, seasons, or March winds.

After a study of kinds of weather, weather facts, and weather words, pass out six butcher-paper strips cut to 21" x 3" (53 x 8 cm) to each student. Each strip should be a different color. The class can then begin making the windsock bodies. Instruct students to illustrate with as many different pictures as possible the following weather categories on the various colored strips: rain, snow, sun, clouds, storms, wind. (The four seasons could be adapted to this idea as well.) Students will enjoy enhancing their pictures with glitter and stars. Have each student glue the six strips edge-to-edge to form a rectangle.

While this dries, pass out six more colored strips cut to 16" x 1 1/2" (40 x 4 cm) for the windsock tails. Have students show how much they know about weather by writing all the weather facts and words they can think of on each tail strip. (Brainstorming together elicits a wealth of ideas.)

When each student is finished, have him or her glue the end of each tail strip to the bottom of the windsock body.

Next, have students roll the windsocks and glue the sides together to make cylinder shapes. Have them add yarn handles, and the windsocks are ready to decorate your classroom.

Your students will love "flying" home with their beautiful creations.

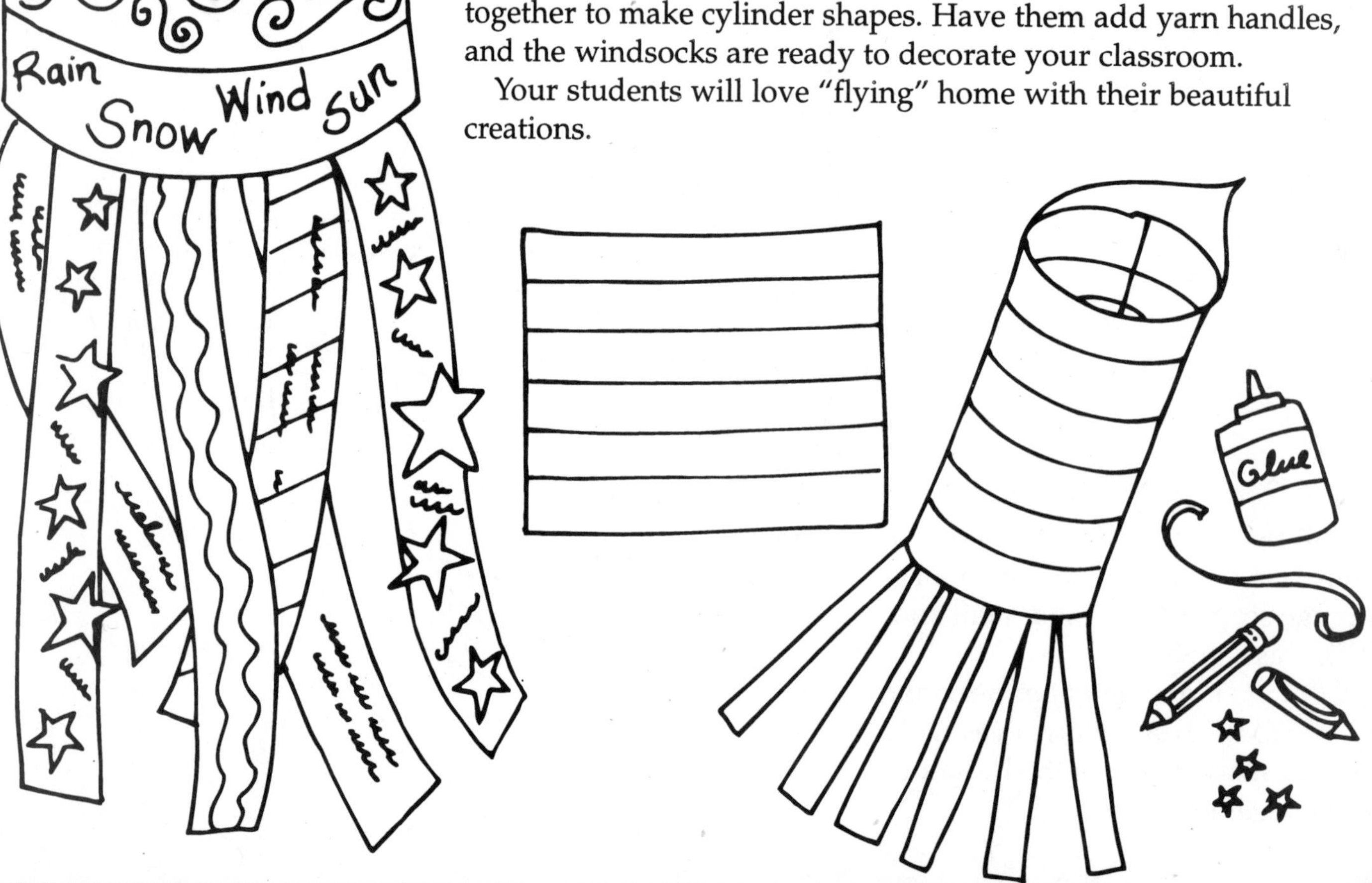

A Sweet May Day Basket

Materials
- one berry basket
- a few lollipops with straight sticks
- plastic foam or clay
- real or artificial flowers and greenery
- black marker
- yarn
- construction paper
- tape

Directions

On each cellophane lollipop wrapper, draw a smiling face with the marker. (Do not draw on the candy!) Tape a real or artificial flower on each lollipop like a hat. Tie a yarn bow under each lollipop face.

Fit foam (or clay) into the bottom of the berry basket. Construction-paper strips can be woven along the sides of the berry basket if you wish. Now push the lollipop sticks into the foam or clay with the "flower people" facing out. Push a few sprigs of greenery around the lollipops and add a yarn bow to the basket. Your May basket is ready to give!

Teepees

Materials
- paper sacks
- crayons
- toothpicks
- glue
- tempera paint (brown)

Directions

1. Soak the sacks in water until the seams open. Then crumple them up and squeeze out the excess water. Carefully smooth them out and let dry.
2. After the sacks have dried, cut out semicircle shapes and draw on Native American designs with crayons. Be sure to press hard! Paint over the designs with a thin coat of brown tempera paint.
3. When the paint has dried, glue toothpicks poking out of the top in the center of the straight side. Fold over the semicircle so it will form a cone and staple or glue the edges near the top. Fold over the bottom flap to give an appearance of a door or small opening.

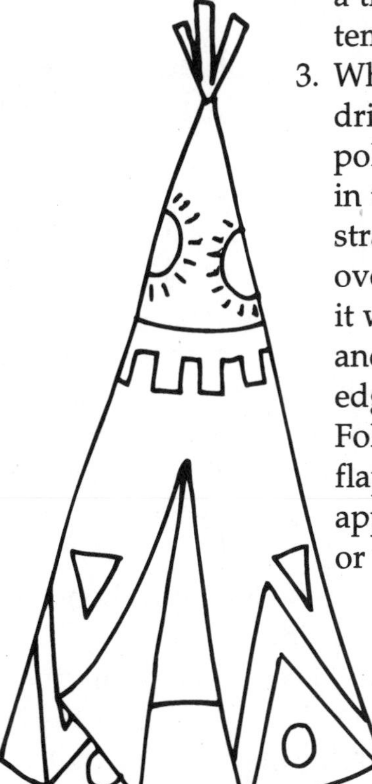

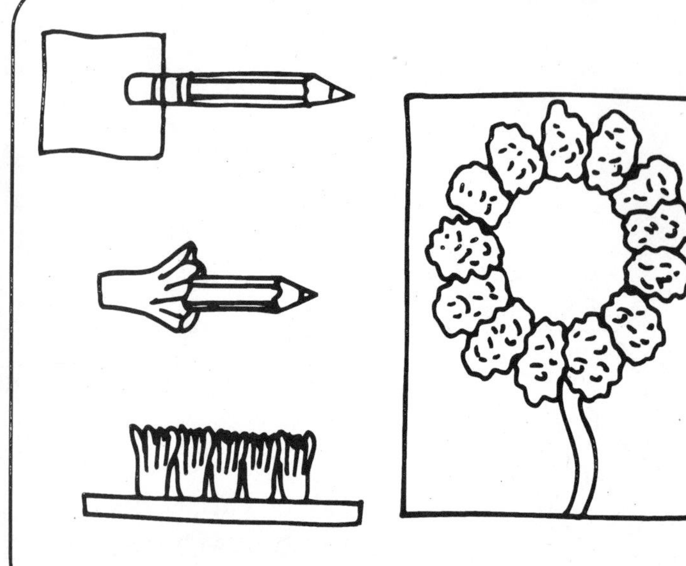

Sunflower Tissue-Paper Art

Directions

1. Reproduce a pattern for a sunflower.
2. Have a lot of pieces of brown and yellow tissue paper cut into 2" x 2" (5 x 5 cm) squares.
3. Wrap a tissue paper square around the eraser of a pencil and dip it lightly into glue. Press the glued tip onto the pattern—brown in the center and yellow on the petals. Continue placing tissue paper around the pattern until all of the white paper is covered. Tissue paper should be placed close together.
4. A stem and background can be added to complete the project.

A School Bookmark

Go outdoors and find two small flowers and two small leaves. To add variety to the bookmark, try to find different colored flowers. Lay a heavy book on the flowers and leaves overnight to flatten them.

Using two sheets of clear adhesive paper, place the flattened flowers and leaves on one sheet's sticky side. Be sure to keep the flowers and leaves within a 2 1/2" (6 cm) wide and 5 1/2" (14 cm) long space.

Press the second sheet of adhesive paper, sticky-side down, on top of the first sheet. They should now be firmly stuck together with the leaves and flowers showing through.

Cut a 2 1/2" (6 cm) wide and 5 1/2" (14 cm) long rectangle around the flowers and leaves. If pinking shears are used, the edges of the bookmark will appear jagged.

Punch a small hole at the top of the bookmark, using either a hole punch or the pointy end of a pair of scissors.

Finally, thread a 12" (30 cm) piece of narrow ribbon through the hole. Bring the two ends together so each side is 6" (15 cm) long. Tie the two ends together, placing the knot near the hole.

The bookmark is finished and ready for the first day of school. Use it yourself or give it to a friend.

Circus Animals

Materials

- 12" x 12" (30 x 30 cm) white paper
- two sheets of 4" x 12" (10 x 30 cm) colored construction paper
- 1/4" x 12" (.4 x 30 cm) black construction paper strips for bars
- two 3" x 3" (8 x 8 cm) sheets of colored construction paper for wheels
- crayons and markers
- watercolors and water dish
- glue and scissors

Directions

1. Discuss with students the animals you would find in cages at a circus.
2. On the 12" x 12" (30 x 30 cm) white paper, have each student draw a large animal (to fill the cage) in crayon. When the drawing is completed, paint with watercolors.
3. The two 4" x 12" (10 x 30 cm) pieces of colored construction paper are the top and bottom of the cage. Design these with decorative, colorful patterns. Use both markers and crayons.
4. Glue bars on top of the animal when watercolor is dry. Don't use too many, as you don't want to cover up the animal.
5. Glue the top and bottom of the cage onto the picture of the animal. These should extend past the top and bottom of the white 12" x 12" (30 x 30 cm) paper.
6. Cut out the wheels. Glue underneath the bottom of the cage.
7. These can be left as is or put into a circus train on a mural, with a string connecting the cages.

Classroom Art Award

To create a mood of achievement for your art room, use this art award. This award is presented to one classroom in the building per week for being the best classroom to visit the art room. The classroom keeps this award for one week, proudly displaying it in their room or on the classroom door. At the end of the week, the art award is returned to the art room and another superior classroom will be selected the following week. A chart is kept and, at the end of the year, the room winning the award the most times receives a special treat. (This concept could be used in any special classroom.)

Teacher Helper: To aid in keeping the art room a cleaner and neater room, grocery bags are attached to the desks to serve as trash cans. With this many trash containers available in one room, cleanup can be faster with less movement around the room. At the end of the week, the bags are dumped and reattached to the desks with masking tape.

Potpourri Containers

Throwaway items can often be recycled into useful, attractive objects. For example, the little plastic baskets that are hung in automatic dishwashers to prevent water spots on dishes can be made into pretty potpourri containers.

Wrap a small amount of your favorite fragrant dried flower and/or herb potpourri in a small square of nylon net, and place it inside one of the little plastic baskets. Now all you need to do is decorate the exterior of the little basket. You can use bits of lace, ribbon, tiny silk flowers, or other trims to make the basket as pleasing to the eye as the potpourri is pleasing to the nose.

Don't overlook the possibility of decorating these potpourri containers in holiday colors and adding them to gift-wrapped presents.

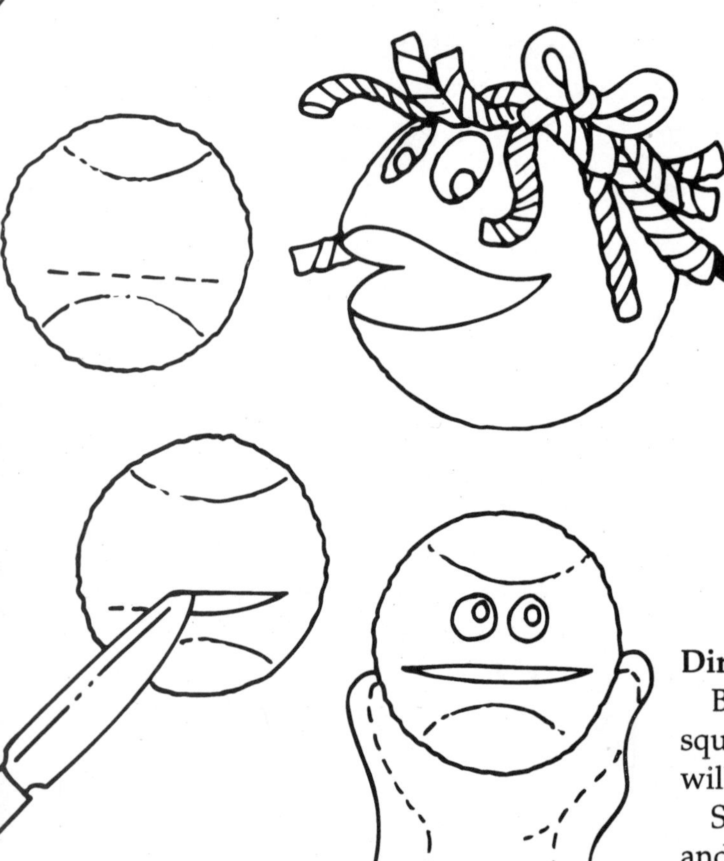

Fun and Easy Puppets

These puppets are easily made, and each one can be given an individual appearance. They are very versatile and can be used by very young children.

Materials

- old tennis balls (ask P.E. teachers, country clubs, or sports clubs)
- sharp carpet cutter or very sharp knife (adult use only)
- black, brown, or blue felt-tip markers
- one 1' (.30 m) square of cloth for each puppet
- yarn (hair colors)
- glue

Directions

Before class, cut tennis balls as shown. By squeezing gently on the sides of the ball, the mouth will open.

Student can draw the eyes using felt-tip makers and attach hair with glue. A square piece of cloth can be draped about the hand of the puppeteer who tucks the ends of cloth into his or her hand.

How to Make a Pile of Junk

Recycling has never been more important than it is now. Landfills are filling at an alarming rate, so it is necessary for us to teach our children about the importance of recycling.

Would you like to show students how to make an interesting statement about life? How about teaching them how to make a junk-pile paperweight? This is a fun and easy project that will give you and your students hours of fun as well as serve as a great conversation piece.

Here is how you can make a "pile of junk" from various items collected around home and school.

Supplies

- pieces of waxed paper to work on
- white craft glue
- shoeboxes to store supplies in
- lid from a wide-mouthed jar

Collect your "junk" (any or all of the following)

- packing pellets
- rubber bands
- paper clips
- empty glue bottles
- empty tape rolls
- old pens/pencils
- beads from broken bracelets or necklaces
- washers and nuts
- small pieces of wood
- Mom's old costume jewelry
- twist ties from bread bags

Directions

1. Divide all "junk" into separate shoeboxes.
2. Place your jar lid on the waxed paper. This will be the base of your paperweight.
3. Start by filling the bottom of the lid first, gluing any of your "junk" to it. After the base is covered, continue to pile and glue items on so that your paperweight grows wide as well as tall. Just be careful not to make your project too tall. Remember the glue needs time to dry and the paperweight will topple if it gets too tall.

In short, any item which is no bigger than a child's hand and is safe and clean to handle may be used. Just when students think they've collected enough "junk," they will find something else to add to their "junk" piles. And when these are put on display, your students will be sure to get many comments and compliments.

Reading Vocabulary Words

As a different approach to learning and displaying vocabulary words, make a vocabulary string mobile. When new words are introduced, each student gets a word and a card. Instruct each student to put the word in large print on one side of the card and a picture showing the meaning of the word on the other side. (This can also include a written definition, if you wish.) Then punch a hole in the bottom and the top of the card and string it on a long shoestring or a piece of yarn with tape wrapped around the end for easier lacing. Students can then stand at the mobiles and practice their words or just see them as they hang in the room.

Springtime Haiku

Teach your students to write haiku by giving them the formula "5-7-5," emphasizing that haiku are usually about nature and stressing that poems don't have to rhyme. Read many examples to them and then write some original ones together.

Later, "pass the hat" containing strips of paper with nature subjects written on them, for example, *cloud, caterpillar, sunbeam, rainbow,* and *nest*. Each student picks one and writes an original haiku on that subject. After the haiku is perfected, have students use construction paper and draw and cut out cherry blossom shapes or shapes symbolic of their subjects. Next, have them neatly copy their haiku onto the cut-outs. Mount the haiku on the branches of a Japanese-style construction-paper cherry tree. (Be sure to explain the significance of cherry trees in the Japanese culture.)

The Three Little "Es" and the Wolf

Display pig silhouettes (use plain cards if time is limited) with "e" words printed on them. Point to a word. Make houses out of shoeboxes showing examples of the various sounds of "e" (see example). If a student can pronounce it and puts the word safely into the right house, the wolf doesn't get the word. The house door can have an envelope, or other container, for the word cards.

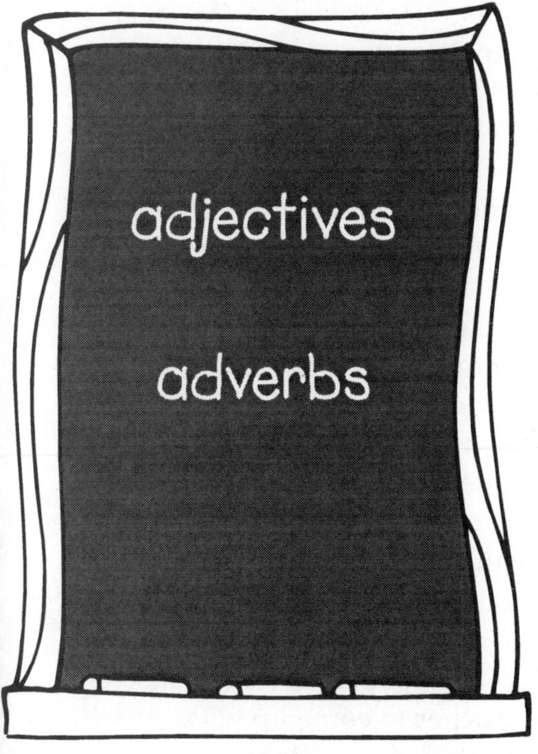

Add-an-Adjective Game

This is a group game that can be used to reinforce adjective or adverb knowledge and use. All that is needed is a chalkboard and chalk!

Directions

To play, a student names one word to start a sentence. The next student says a second word in the sentence, and so on. When one sentence ends, another can be started. Each word is written on the chalkboard. If the word given is an adjective or adverb, the player must say his or her word and then label it with the correct part of speech.

Points are awarded for words that are adjectives or adverbs: one point for adjectives, two points for adverbs. Only three consecutive adjectives or adverbs can be used. One point is subtracted for incorrect labeling. The teacher determines accuracy. The winner is the player with the highest score. Individual or team scores can be kept to see who is the lucky adjective and adverb champion!

Try this game with other parts of speech to reinforce those as well!

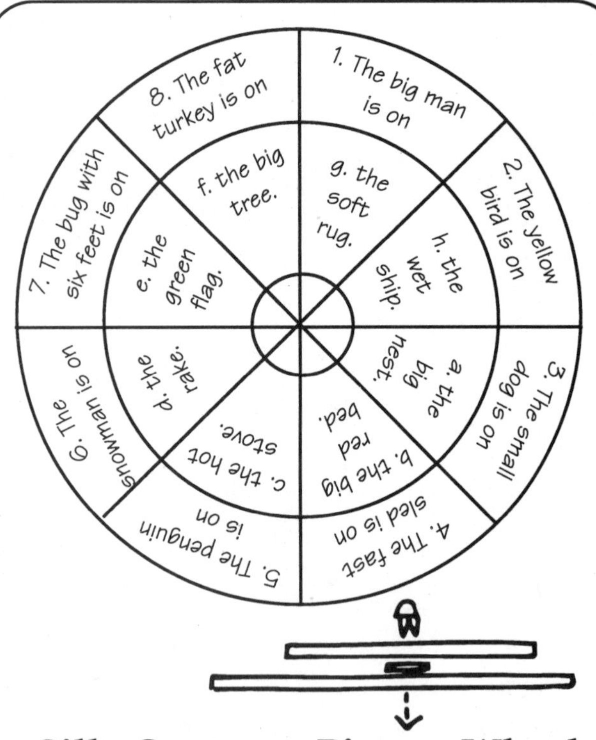

Silly Sentence Picture Wheel

The purpose of this activity is to allow independent phonics practice in which students can show their ability to sound out words.

Materials

- 1 large pizza board
- 1 small pizza board
- markers
- paper fastener
- washer

Method

Each student spins the inner wheel. Then he or she writes down a corresponding number and letter on a piece of drawing paper. (This will enable the teacher to check the drawing at a later time.) The student then sounds out the silly sentence formed by the combined wheels and draws a picture of the sentence. The student's drawing tells the teacher if he or she has correctly sounded out the sentence.

The Great Snowflake Race

For developing an interest in research and encyclopedia usage, have a Great Snowflake Race. Post a chart on the wall with every student's name on it and numbers from 1-50.

Place 50 construction-paper snowflakes in a can. Each snowflake is numbered and contains a question. For example, "Who was the third president of the U.S. and when was he elected to the position?" "Name three requirements for a candidate for the presidency." "Who was the largest president?" "Which president had the most children?" Students must answer each question satisfactorily in order to put a star in the box for that question. The activity is a race to see who can complete all 50 questions first and have all 50 boxes starred beside his or her name on the chart.

(A number of topics can be used for this activity, and it is up to the teacher to come up with questions that will be appropriate for each class.)

Word Walls

Cover an expanse of wall in the classroom with white paper. Ask students to think of compound words which contain *moon*. Write them on the wall. Examples: *moonbeam, moonlight, honeymoon,* and so on. Or ask students for words that rhyme with *moon*. Examples: *soon, June, croon,* and so on.

Stories in Sequence

Writing a class story is interesting and fun. Every writer, whether a great author or just a beginner, writes stories with a beginning, middle, and an end.

Your class can become a collective author with this fun exercise. Number each class member alphabetically by last name or by birth date, one through the number in class. After the class members have numbers, pass out cards with matching numbers. Number one writes a sentence or paragraph on his or her card and reads it to the class. Number two picks up the story and adds his or her sentence or paragraph. The activity continues until the last student ends the story. When all cards have been read, place them in sequence around the room and leave them up for two or three days for everyone to enjoy.

"I Am" Poems

"I Am" poems, in which students write about themselves, are a good exercise to spark an interest in poetry. Place all the poems, unsigned, on a bulletin board and have class members write the name of the person who they think wrote each poem. The poem(s) with the greatest number of correct identifications will be declared the winner. Poems should emphasize characteristics and feelings rather than physical descriptions such as tall, short, red hair, and so on.

Pattern

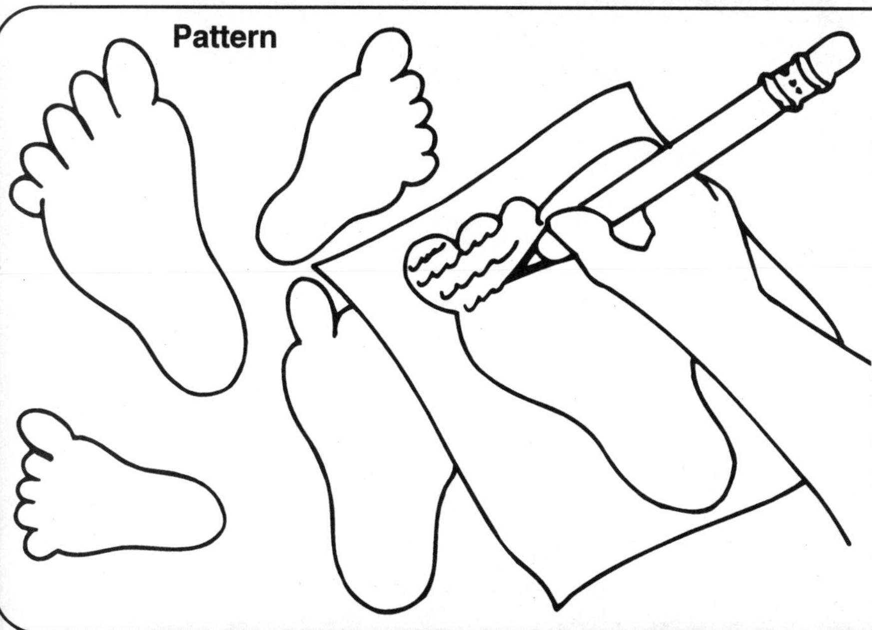

Whose Prints Are Those?

Enlarge the footprint pattern provided and make several copies. Place these footprints around the room in a path along the ceiling, down and across the wall, over the chalkboard, and into desks and tote trays.

Then brainstorm several possibilities of who made the prints and how they got there. Each student then writes a story on an 8 1/2" x 11" sheet of paper (as shown).

Later, have students create the creature that they think left the footprints.

Create a Snowman

To encourage students to read more during the long winter months, start this project in January. Each student should make the basic form of a snowman (head, middle, body). These pictures are then placed on a wall. Each student must read six books by the first day of spring, and he or she must write a book report on each book. After a report is corrected, each student may add a feature to his or her snowman. The following features can be used.

1st book—eyes
2nd book—nose
3rd book—mouth
4th book—arms
5th book—hat
6th book—scarf

When, and if, a student finishes the sixth book, he or she picks from the Goodie Jar. If a student does not finish the six book reports, he or she must pick from the Jobs Jar. The Goodie Jar has special reward notes such as 10 fewer math problems, a half-hour extra library time, a half-hour free time, and so on. The Jobs Jar assigns extra tasks such as picking paper up off the floor, completing 10 extra math problems, and so on.

The Reading Railroad

The purpose of the reading railroad is to motivate library reading and book reports. After reading a book, a student writes the following on an index card: title, author, what the book was about, and what he or she liked about the book. The index card is glued on a "car" of the train. The cards are attached to an engine and hung on the wall. Each student may read as many books as he or she wants; thus the train "grows" until it circles the room. Emphasize cooperation to make the train longer rather than competition to see who can read the most books.

Reading Rainbow

Using 9" x 12" sheets of colored construction paper, make a rainbow on one of your bulletin boards. Each sheet of construction paper should show a space for a book report. The challenge to the entire class is to fill the rainbow with book reports (or math skills sheets, etc.).

When the rainbow is full, a treat will be found in the pot at the end of the rainbow. The treat can be a favorite classroom game, a popcorn party, a favorite game in the gym, or time for a walking field trip.

Fun With Vowels and Syllables

These two manipulatives are a great way for students to learn more about syllables and vowel sounds. They can be seasonal (as shown here) or simply made using any catalog or old workbook pictures.

Using any size pizza board, glue on appropriate pictures and words for each game. Title one board "Name that Vowel" and the other "Count the Syllables." Print the answers on the back in the corresponding place. Cover with clear contact paper or laminate.

To play, students use a clothespin to clip the pictures they choose. They then say the number of syllables or the vowel sounds they hear in the word that names the picture. Their answers are checked by turning the board over.

Paperback Book Club

Most students have good collections of paperback books at home that they may wish to share with their classmates. In order to do this, start a PBB Club (Paperback Book Club). Print the rules on a large poster and hang it in the area of the PBB Club shelves, away from the regular classroom books. Your class will probably come up with some different rules, but these can be used as a guide:

1. Each participant may bring only six books at a time.
2. Each month we will bring six different books and take home the previous set.
3. Lost or destroyed books will be replaced with a book of equal value.
4. Books will be kept at school unless written permission to take the book home is given by the book owner.

This is a great way for students to learn about accepting responsibility for other people's property and the value of being trusted by classmates.

Student Journal

Keeping a journal is a good way to practice putting thoughts on paper. Have students keep a journal or log for one week or more. Here are some ideas to get them started: Write a sentence or two about your family, the weather, what you ate, where you went, your feelings, disappointing or happy events, your best friend, or a new friend.

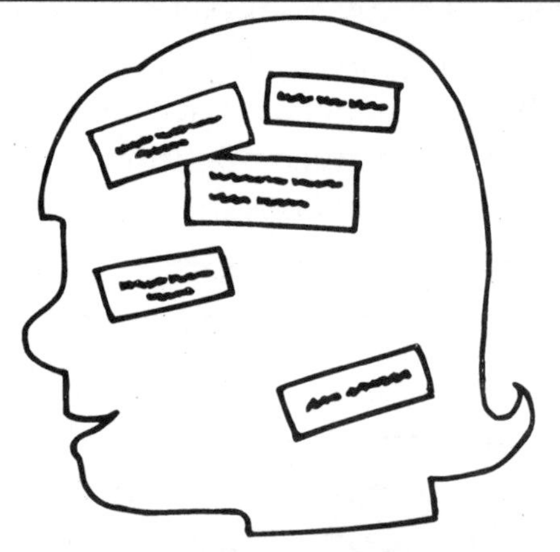

Fill Your Head!

Help each student draw a large profile of his or her head by making a silhouette on the wall with a projector or lamp. Trace the outline of the head, cut it out, and place it on the bulletin board. Make a vocabulary list for each student. When a student can pronounce and spell a word correctly for two consecutive days, he or she writes that particular word on a piece of oaktag and glues or pins it on the bulletin board silhouette. This activity is a great way to chart new words learned during a grading period.

Three Colorful Cousins

Most students love candy, and M&M's™ candies are favorites. You can use this colorful candy to aid in teaching students about the three M's of our language: Homonyms, Antonyms, and Synonyms.

Purchase a large package of M&M's™ candies. Separate them into colors, placing each color in a separate container. Decide on the three colors you want to use for this activity. Assign a color to each of the "-nym" words. (Do not use this activity until all the "-nyms" have been studied in class.)

After all three word types have been studied and reviewed, prepare a worksheet or a game activity that uses these three cousins. Prepare different worksheets for each group or even each student. Write 12 sentences with "nyms" in them on each worksheet. Laminate your sheets so they can be used over and over again. Give each student or group containers of the three colors of M&M's candies that correspond with the "nym" color codes you have used throughout the study. The candies will be used to identify which "nyms" were used in the activities you have prepared. You may wish to have the color codes on the worksheet or somewhere in the language center as a reminder.

To complete the activities, give each group or student an egg carton bottom. Write a number in each cup of the carton. The number corresponds to the number of each sentence. Since there are 12 cups per carton, each worksheet should have up to 12 sentences.

Read the sentences and have students decide which of the three cousins has been used. For example, for "I would not like to be a bee!," two M&M's candies representing the homonym color are placed in the cup that corresponds to the sentence.

When all sentences have been completed, have students check their work by using an answer key in the shape of an egg carton. Each cup should contain colored dots to indicate the answers. After checking, students can enjoy the candies as a treat.

The Creative Writing Challenge

Materials

- several large plastic foam or paper cups on which to write the story starters
- a ditto of a large cup for students to write their stories on

Teacher Directions

Print story starters on cups and tack the cups to the bulletin board. Have the dittoed-cup paper or other paper available.

Student Directions

1. Read the story starters on the cups. Choose one and write a story on the paper that is provided.
2. Put your story in the cup when you are finished.
3. Read a couple of the other stories that are in the cups.

Possible Story Starters

1. The drink in the cup was deep red, cool, and very delicious. I drank half the cup without stopping. Suddenly I felt strange. I looked at my foot and . . .
2. I work in a paper cup factory. My boss wants new uses for paper cups. I think paper cups could be used for . . .
3. The cup was blowing in the wind across the deserted beach. I picked it up and looked inside. My eyes popped, and I screamed as I saw . . .
4. My name is Quarf, and I am from the planet Neptune. As I step out of my spaceship, I find a paper cup. I look with my photo eyes, and I can see everywhere this cup has been. This is what I see . . .

English Review Game

Cut 13 regular-sized white envelopes in half and glue them onto a large sheet of posterboard, making five rows of five envelope halves. Number each row 10, 20, 30, 40, and 50 to designate point value. List five different categories on the board above the columns of envelopes: Dictionary, Parts of Speech, Poetry, Capitalization and Punctuation, Take a Chance.

Questions ranging in difficulty are written on index cards, which are then placed in the envelope pockets. Make some questions as bonus questions (double points). Teams compete by choosing any category and point value. The winner is the team with the most points.

Language Arts

The Spelling Challenge

Teacher Directions

Put current spelling list words or other spelling words on cups (10–15 words). Spell the word correctly on one cup and spell it incorrectly on another cup. Set the cups side by side. Have students place a straw in the cup with the correctly spelled word.

Student Directions

Place a straw in every cup with a correctly spelled word printed on it. Do not put straws in the cups with incorrectly spelled words.

Possible Spelling Starters

rabbit-rabit
hitting-hiting
picture-picksure
double-doubel
library-librery
parties-partys
enough-enuff
knife-nife
taking-takeing
giggling-giggleing
said-siad
cheer-chear

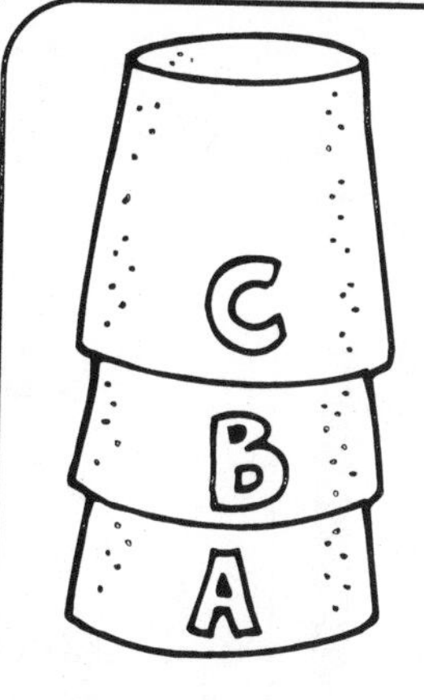

ABC C

Teacher Direct

Print words o current spelling or voca use the challenging list below. the cups in random order. Have students unstack the cups and restack them in ABC order.

Student Directions

Restack the cups, putting the words in ABC order. The "A" word will be on the bottom.

Possible Word List

appropriate	beneficial	courteous	delicious
extraterrestrial	ferocious	generous	horrible
juicy	kindred	likable	magnificent
numerous	omnipotent	pleasant	quickly
rational	sensational	terrific	universal
wonderful	young		

Name That Character!

Put your budding young detectives to work guessing the identity of popular book characters. The characters can either be people or animals. Here is a list of ideas: Heidi, Alice in Wonderland, Cinderella, Miss Nelson, Mary Poppins, Curious George, Winnie the Pooh, Babar, Clifford the Big Red Dog, and Corduroy. Write each book character's name on a small index card. Divide your class into teams of four or five students and have a team captain choose one of the character cards. (Ssh! It's a secret!) Have each team meet quietly and write five one-word clues about the character or book. For example, clue words for Cinderella could be: ball, pumpkin, stepmother, work, prince. Set an appropriate time limit for the teams to meet.

When time is up, have a sharing time. Let the audience guess the mystery characters by using the clues given by each team.

Be a Detective!

To further extend the previous activity, turn each team into a detective agency. Have each team captain choose one of the book character cards. Each team will then meet quietly and choose a make-believe name for the detective agency. They will pretend that the book character on their card is missing, and their agency will solve the mystery. First, have them list any clues found at the scene of the crime. (If desired, each team can be given a Super Sleuth Clue Box with small clues, such as buttons, and pieces of thread, or students can make up their own clues.) Next, have them write a "crime report" or skit telling how their detective agency solved the mystery of the missing character. Have each team share its completed work with the class.

Learning Center

Teacher Tips

Chilly Chores

Using the snowman pattern and the activities found below, make a wintertime learning center for your classroom.

Reproduce the pattern and type or write one activity on each snowman. Laminate for lasting durability.

- If Frosty the Snowman came to your house to spend the day, what are some things that you would do?
- Describe and draw a new invention that removes snow from the sidewalk without using a shovel.
- Make a list of all the different board games you can think of that would be fun to play in the winter.
- Make a list of all the winter sports you can think of.
- Make a word search containing at least 20 words that pertain to winter.
- Design a snowman using plastic foam pieces. Name it and write a short poem about it.
- Write five synonyms for *cold*. Write five antonyms for *cold*. Choose one of each and use them in a winter sentence.
- Pick your favorite winter sport and write directions for playing it. Read your directions to a friend and see if he or she can draw a picture using your directions.
- Use the encyclopedia to find out how snowflakes are formed. Design one of your own on paper and cut it out.
- List 20 words that remind you of winter.

Put a phone book in a learning center. Write the following questions on a folder or a sheet of paper.

1. What number would you call if someone in your house was sick and needed an ambulance?
2. What number would you call if your house was on fire?
3. What number would you call if you heard a prowler outside?
4. What number would you call if you needed to call the operator?
5. What number would you call if your phone was out of order?
6. What is your area code?
7. What is meant by a person-to-person call?
8. What is meant by a station-to-station call?
9. How is your phone number listed?
10. How many different cities or towns are listed in the phone book?
11. What are the most expensive times to make long distance calls?
12. What are the least expensive times to make long distance calls?
13. How many people have the same last name as you?

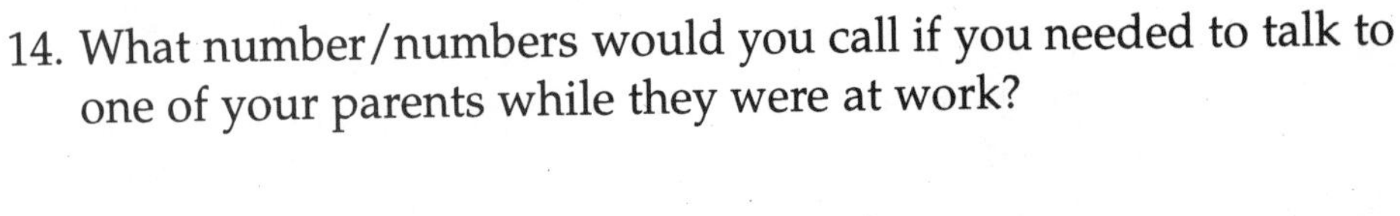

14. What number/numbers would you call if you needed to talk to one of your parents while they were at work?

Canned Questions and Answers

When apples and other fruits and vegetables ripen in the fall, canning becomes an important activity for many families. Many of your students probably have had some firsthand experience with what canning is all about.

In your classroom, let students experience some academic "canning." This activity can be used for individual students, group research, class involvement within one discipline, or within the context of many subject areas you are covering in class.

Purchase a case or two of canning jars. Decide what fruits and/or vegetables you want to "can" for this activity. Choose construction paper in colors similar to the colors of the real fruits and/or vegetables you have chosen for this activity (example: purple for grapes, yellow for corn, and so on). Decide on a place in your classroom that can be used as the "pantry."

Outline the shapes of your chosen vegetables and/or fruits. Make them large enough to write questions on but small enough to fit into your canning jars. Cut out each one and write questions, directions, math problems, and so on, on each. Each piece of fruit can have one activity or question, or if you are dealing with one article or story from a basal reader, more than one question can be written. If possible, laminate each piece of fruit and/or vegetable before placing it in the jar. (Label each piece with a different letter or number.)

Place the fruit and/or vegetables in the jars and arrange them on the "pantry" shelf. Perhaps you would want to label each jar with titles such as *Corny Questions*, or *Grape Research Activities*. Use your imagination.

Next, design a worksheet that students will use to write their answers on when they have completed their research. Perhaps an outline of a large jar with lines drawn on the front would work.

Place several copies of the worksheet in the pantry area. Students then choose a jar, pick a fruit or vegetable, and answer the question. Make sure that students label each answer sheet with the letter or number you have used to label the fruit. This will keep a record of the fruits and vegetables "eaten."

Have students line up their answer "jars" on a bulletin board or in a straight line on a wall of the classroom. Share and discuss the results when time permits.

Category Game

To help students become more aware of words that denote categories, as well as words that make up categories, try this game. Choose three students to play together. One student holds a set of alphabet cards and names the categories. Having a set list of categories on hand makes the game go smoother. The other two students vie with each other to be the first to call out a word which falls into the category and which begins with the letter the cardholder holds up. For example, the cardholder calls out the category "Vegetable" while holding up the B card. The other two students race with each other to name a vegetable that starts with the letter B. They could say *bean, broccoli,* or *beet.* The first player who gives an appropriate word beginning with the shown letter and in the stated category receives a point. The player who gets the most points during the playing time wins the game.

This game calls for quick thinking and recall. Some students begin to look in their dictionaries for unusual and different words to spring on their classmates. They become more word conscious and increase the number of words in their vocabularies.

Learning Centers

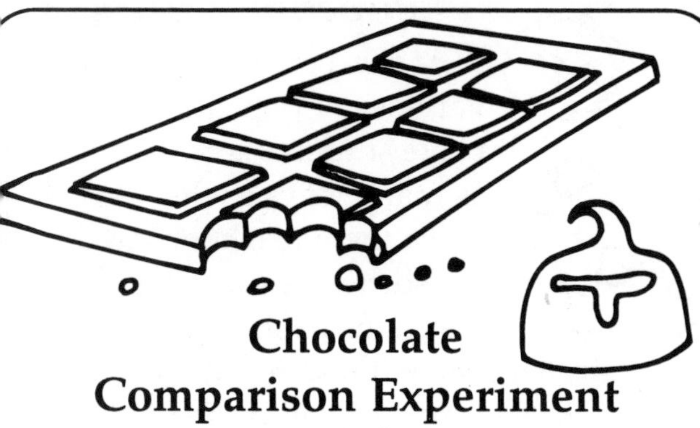

Chocolate Comparison Experiment

Have students devise an experiment or survey in which they test various brands of chocolate for taste, appearance, smell, and so on. Have them conduct their experiment and report the results, using graphs and charts, to show what they have discovered.

Charlie and the Chocolate Factory

Have students read or listen to excerpts from *Charlie and the Chocolate Factory* by Roald Dahl. Have them use Charlie as the main character in a cooperative story, adding another chapter to the book.

How Chocolate Came to Be

At this center, include information about how chocolate really came to be. Also include examples of myths and legends which explain how the bear got its short tail or how the turtle got its shell or how thunder was invented. Have students brainstorm many varied and unusual explanations for how chocolate came to be. Have them create a script for their most original idea and act it out for the class.

It's a New Taste Sensation

At this center, provide examples of a wide variety of chocolate products. Have students create their own original chocolate products and design an ad campaign for selling these products. Have them videotape their finished ads. Have students vote on the videos and award a prize for the top new chocolate product.

Learning Centers

Popcorn Galore!

At this center, have students work together to brainstorm all the possible varieties of popcorn they can create. Have them list these varieties. Then have them select the best idea and prepare a marketing plan for this new, improved popcorn.

Popcorn Critics

At this center, have several varieties of popcorn kernels. Have students sort these in as many ways as they can. Have them use hoops to do the sorting and use Venn diagrams to show their results. Have students share these results with the rest of the class. Scales, magnifying glasses, various measuring utensils, and other devices should be placed at this center. A popcorn popper should also be on hand so that students can test their predictions about the best popping results by using small quantities of each variety.

100 Creative Ways to Use Popcorn!

In this center, have students stretch their creative thinking skills by brainstorming a list of at least 100 things to do with popcorn—besides eating it! They may make the popcorn larger, smaller, glue it together, and combine it with other things to come up with new ideas!

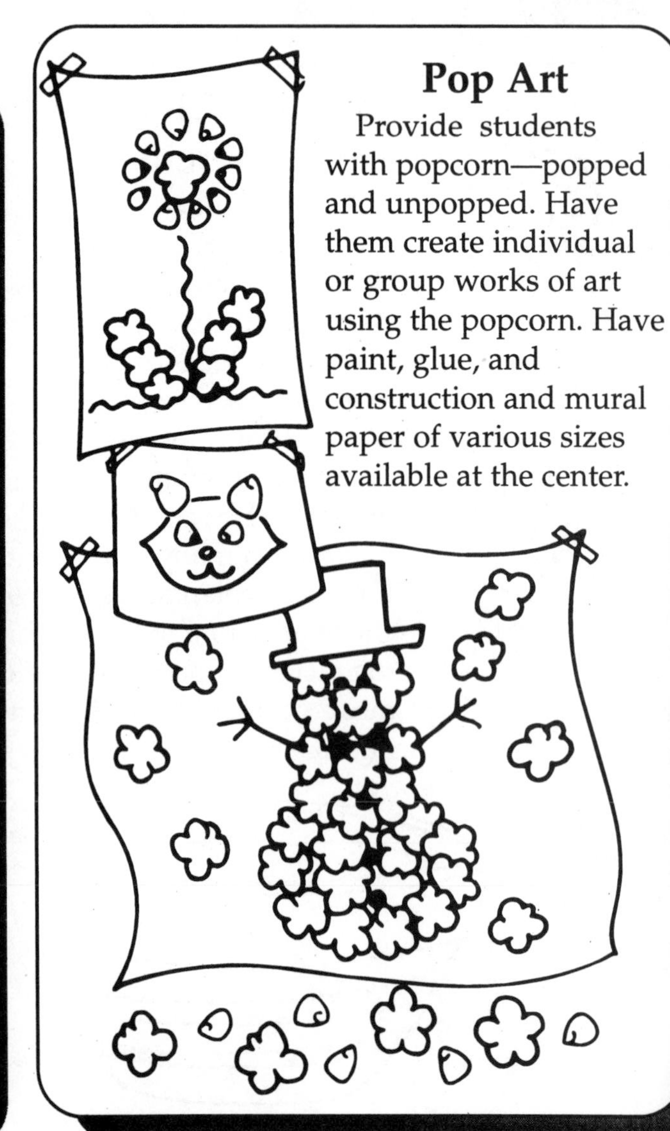

Pop Art

Provide students with popcorn—popped and unpopped. Have them create individual or group works of art using the popcorn. Have paint, glue, and construction and mural paper of various sizes available at the center.

Social Studies

Tell students to select any foreign country. Ask them to imagine they had to send a greeting card to someone in that country wishing them a happy May Day or any other holiday. What type of picture should be on the front of the card? What greetings should be included? Have students fold large sheets of art paper to make and decorate cards. When the cards are completed, use a large world map to locate countries for which the cards have been created.

Loads of Logs

Cut quite a few "Lincoln Logs" from brown posterboard or cardboard. Print a task relating to Abraham Lincoln on each of them for the students to complete. (It might be a good idea to have some books on Abraham Lincoln readily available for students to use in the classroom.) Some examples of tasks are given below, but feel free to make up many more of your own in order to adapt them more specifically to the students. When all the tasks are completed, the class could get together and write a research paper about the life of Abraham Lincoln.

Store the logs in a can covered with black sticky paper and with a round piece of black posterboard or cardboard glued to the bottom of the can to resemble a hat worn by Lincoln.

Geography Fun

For a real test of your students' resourcefulness, have them go on a Seasonal Geography Hunt. The object is to find a winter-related city, mountain, lake, river, landmark, and so on, in every state. It can even be the state itself, such as Washington (February). Other winter examples include: Lincoln, Nebraska; Snowmass Mountain in Colorado; or Lake Placid, New York (site of the 1980 Winter Olympics). Provide maps, almanacs, encyclopedias—anything that can be used as reference. This could even be turned into a contest with the student having the most answers at the end of the designated time limit being the winner.

Capital Match

Materials

- shoebox
- cards
- glue
- old U.S. puzzle
- old U.S. map
- gummed stars
- wooden craft sticks
- small juice can
- colored sticky paper

Preparations

1. Glue the states from an old U.S. puzzle on the cards. Put the names of the state capitals on the backs.
2. Color the tips of wooden sticks either red, white, or blue.
3. Cover a juice can with colored sticky paper.
4. Make a card that says, Red—1 card, White—2 cards, Blue—3 cards.
5. Provide gummed stars for awards. Store everything in a shoebox that has been covered with states cut from old maps.

Directions

1. Take out the can and sticks. Put the colored ends of the sticks into the bottom of the can.
2. Take out the color-code card but leave the state cards in the shoebox. Make sure that they are answer side down.
3. Player 1 draws a stick from the can. If he draws a red stick, he gets to draw one state card from the box. If he correctly names the capital, he keeps the card and puts the stick back into the can. If he does not answer correctly, he puts the state card back into the box.
4. Player 2 then goes. The winner is the one with the most state cards at the end of the game and he or she gets to wear a star.

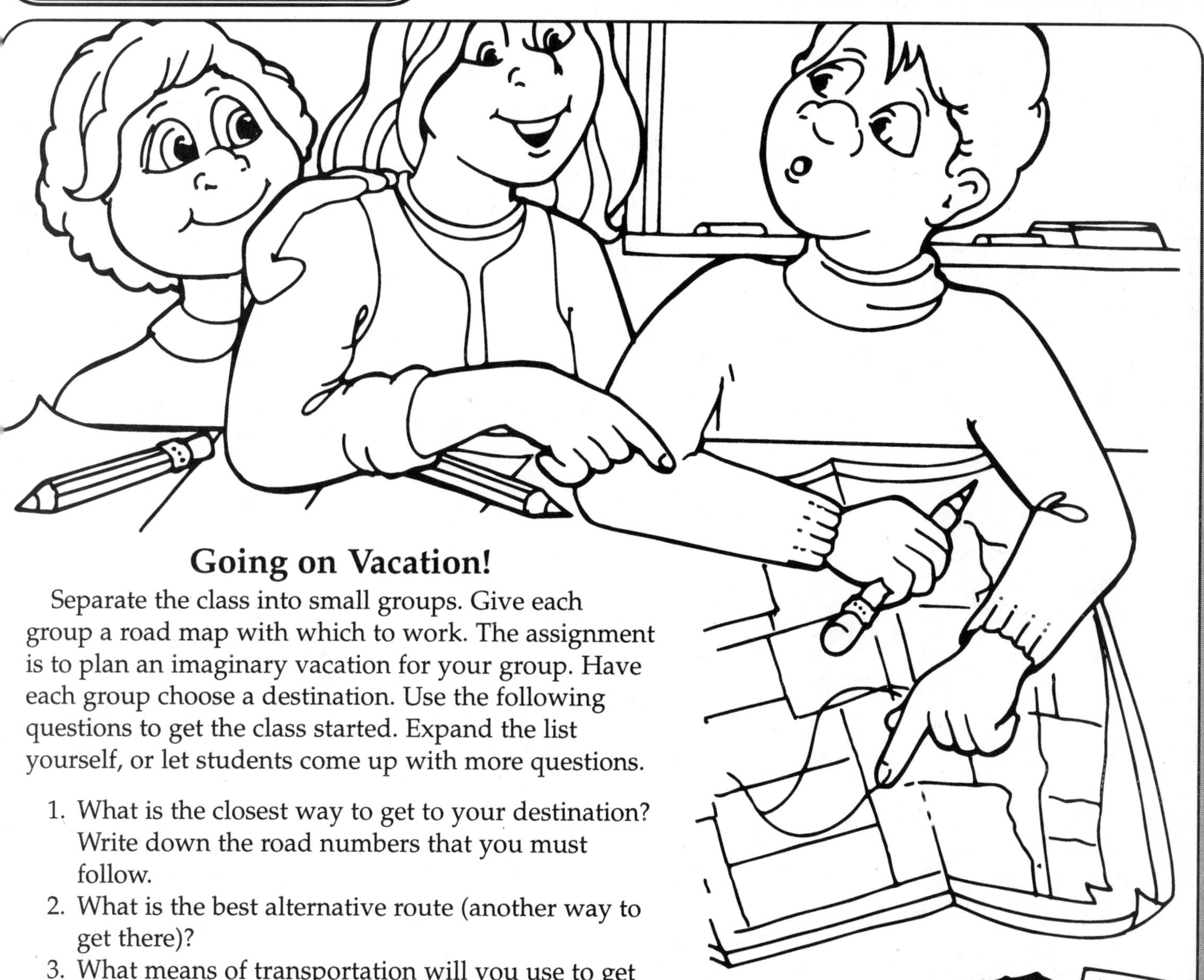

Going on Vacation!

Separate the class into small groups. Give each group a road map with which to work. The assignment is to plan an imaginary vacation for your group. Have each group choose a destination. Use the following questions to get the class started. Expand the list yourself, or let students come up with more questions.

1. What is the closest way to get to your destination? Write down the road numbers that you must follow.
2. What is the best alternative route (another way to get there)?
3. What means of transportation will you use to get to your destination? (plane, train, boat, car)
4. What specific things might you see along the way? (forests, campgrounds, monuments, and so on)
5. How many county lines will you cross over? What counties will you go through?
6. Will you have to cross any state lines? Which ones?
7. Will you stop and rest? Where? For how long?
8. Will you cross any rivers or lakes? Name them.
9. What do you plan to do on your vacation?
10. Whom are you planning to take with you?
11. For this time of year, what kinds of clothes will you pack? Will the weather be the same as it is here?
12. What supplies will you need to take with you?

Learning About the Past

It's sometimes hard for students to relate to people like George Washington or Abraham Lincoln since they lived so long ago. This project will help to bring these men and the times in which they lived into focus.

Write a Newspaper

Write (and make photocopies for other classes) your own "News of the Times." Write it as if everything were happening today. Include famous people in the news, such as "Betsy Ross Starts Sewing Nation's First Flag" or "Lincoln Declares Slavery at an End."

With lots of research, each item will come alive and become a fun and interesting way to review history. Assign half of the class to the Washington paper and half to the Lincoln paper.

Interviews With Washington and Lincoln

Pick two students to portray Washington and Lincoln, and others to be important people connected with their lives (such as Martha Washington and Mary Todd Lincoln).

Stress that everyone must be adequately prepared, since you'll expect the "audience" to be asking important questions that the speakers should be prepared to answer.

Have your Mr. Washington wear a three-sided hat and Mr. Lincoln wear a black stovepipe hat and beard.

Sailing on the *Niña, Pinta,* and *Santa Maria*

Columbus used three ships—the *Niña*, the *Pinta*, and the *Santa Maria*—to explore a new world.

Divide students into groups of three. Show pictures of ships similar to those of this period. Supply students with large cardboard boxes, white fabric or durable paper, a dowel rod for the mast, tape, and art supplies. Have students design their own ships. After the ships are complete, invite another class to view your students' creative talents. Later, place the ships in a reading center for the month of October.

An Interview With Columbus

During your study of this famous explorer, plan an interview with your subject. Guide students to research information about the late 1400s, the life of Columbus, and other historical facts. You may want to assign one student to take the part of Columbus and dress in a costume of this period. Class members may use their questions as a way of gathering information or as a review of the unit.

Journal of My Voyage With Columbus

The world was changed by Columbus and others like him. In proving that the world was round instead of flat, he opened the way for other explorers. Ask students to pretend they are sailors who Columbus convinced to accompany him in search of the New World. Have them keep a journal of their "journey."

Start the first entry on August 3, 1492, and end with October 12, 1492. Suggest students make at least one notation for each week during this time span.

Post these words or phrases to stimulate creative thoughts:

breezes	tide	water
sky	birds	sea monsters
mistake	sour food	stale water
sickness	fear	doubt
hunger	storms	the unknown
branch	land	beach
Indians		

Make Your Own Mountain

With clay, form a mountain. Add trees made from pipe cleaners and flowers made from cardboard. Place the mountain on a wooden surface and make it large enough to carve in paths and rivers. Paint the grassy areas green and brown, and the top white with snow.

United Nations Feast

With the help of parents, prepare a United Nations feast with foods from around the world. Below are some suggested foods your class might try.

Rice (a staple in Asia)
Yams or Sweet Potatoes (Africa)
Bean Cakes (Asia)
Cornmeal Cakes (Central and South America)
Yogurt (Asia)
Pasta (Southern Europe)
Flat Pancakes (Russia)
Cheese (worldwide)

Send invitations for the United Nations celebrations to the principal, school secretary, lunchroom aides, and other school personnel.

United Nations Bulletin Board

Enlarge an outline map of the world. Attach a United Nations label or small flag to as many member nations as you can fit on the map. Following are some of the 185 U.N. members: Argentina, Australia, Belgium, Bolivia, Brazil, Canada, Dominican Republic, Ecuador, Egypt, El Salvador, Ethiopia, France, Greece, Guatemala, Honduras, India, Lebanon, Luxembourg, Mexico, Netherlands, New Zealand, Nicaragua, Norway, Paraguay, United Kingdom, and United States of America.

The hope of the United Nations is that through peaceful discussions, violent conflicts can be avoided. With your students, talk about ways in which they could help keep peace within their class, school, and community. From that discussion, help each student record his or her wish for peace. Record these wishes on strips of blue paper, 2" x 8" (5 x 20 cm) long. Make a paper chain out of the wishes, with every other link being made from plain blue paper. For your bulletin board, form the chain into a circle with the wishes toward the outside, and staple together, attaching the links to the previous round. A 50-link chain will make about a 25" to 28" (64 to 71 cm) circle. Over the blue circle, add a white cutout of the continents. Using the olive leaf pattern, cut out 4 branches and 16 leaves from white paper. Make a vine along the side similar to the one that appears on the United Nations flag. Over the top, write the caption *Peace for Our World Family.*

Math

One Stands Alone

Materials

- 3" x 5" (8 x 13 cm) index cards
- paper fastener
- oaktag
- scissors
- various colors of construction paper

Write a riddle or a math story problem on each card. Make three 1/2" x 3" (1.25 x 8 cm) strips from oaktag for each card. Secure these strips to the right side of the index card with a paper fastener. Use various colors of construction paper and make flower shapes. On these flower shapes, write three answers to the question which is written on the index card. The student reads the problem, raises the three flower strips, and chooses one answer. If correct, an "X" will be on the back of the flower shape. One flower strip will stand and the other two will be folded in back of the card.

Toothpick Geometric Figure Race

- Give each student 10 toothpicks. Call out a geometric figure, such as "pentagon." First student to make a correct pentagon scores a point. The student with the most points wins.

- Or, divide class into teams of five students each. There can be as many teams as necessary. Call out a geometric shape, such as "hexagon." First team to form the shape scores a point.

- Give each student 10 toothpicks. Have each student make a shape as you call it out. There is no contest nor points scored.

- Shapes that can be used, depending on the sophistication of students, include the following: square, triangle, quadrilateral, polygon, right angle, acute angle, obtuse angle, perpendicular lines, parallel lines, hexagon, octagon, and decagon.

	Total
Week 1	37¢
Week 2	14¢
Week 3	52¢
Week 4	
Week 5	

Mathematics

Gather or save large shopping bags from a local market. Divide the class into small groups of two or three to decorate each bag with a spring theme. When bags are completed, tape them to the chalkboard ledge or hang them on a bulletin board low enough for students to reach. Tell them that these bags will be like the wishing wells used in England. (Send notes home so that parents are informed of the project. Ask if they can send just a few pennies for the wishing wells. Explain that the money will be given to the homeless or another needy charity in your area.) At the end of each day, have students count the amount of money in the bags and record these on a large wall graph. At the end of the week, have students add the entire amount collected. Discuss where they think the money should be donated.

Even and Odd Numbers

After discussing even and odd numbers, use the math activities described below to develop worksheets to help reinforce the skill. One idea is to draw several circles on a sheet of paper with three- or four-digit numbers in each of them. Then give the following directions: Add all the even numbers and then add all the odd numbers. Subtract the smaller number from the larger number to find the difference. Alternate directions: Color the even numbers a certain color and the odd numbers another color. These directions could also be combined into one activity sheet rather than two.

The Mice and the Cheese

For drill in addition facts, make paper mice and number them 1 to 10 or however high you want to go with your facts. Make a mouse for each number wanted. Then make cheese for the mice to "eat." Write math sentences on the cheese. For example, for the number 4 mouse you could make a cheese with 4 + 0, 3 + 1, 2 + 2, 1 + 3, or 0 + 4. Write the first number and the plus sign on top of the cheese and punch holes to represent the second number in the equation. Then have students match the cheese to the appropriate mouse. As a variation, hold up a numbered mouse and ask students to write as many equations as they can that would equal the number shown.

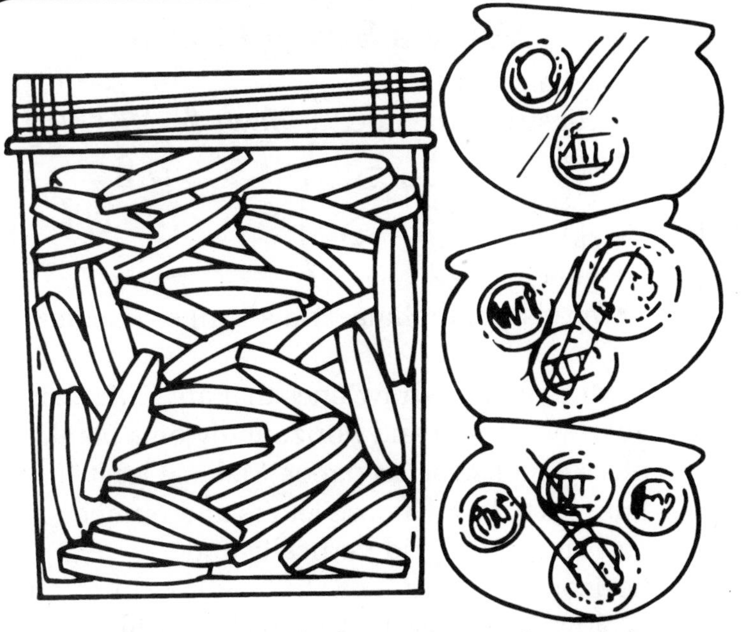

How Much in a Pot of Gold?

Fill a peanut butter jar with pennies. Have students guess the correct number of pennies in the jar. Five new pennies will make a nice prize for the winner. This is an excellent lead-in to a discussion of estimation.

If you have students who have mastered the concept of counting coins, here are some questions that will send them off to the library for some old-fashioned research. Entitle this activity Search for Gold.

- What does 14, 18, and 24 karat gold mean?
- How are gold coins made and where are they made?
- What was the Gold Rush?

Give students practice in counting money by using paper pots of gold. Cut out 10 pots from sheets of golden colored construction paper. On each paper pot, stamp a variety of coins. Use coin stamps and a stamp pad to make this task easy. Place all the completed "pots of gold" in a pocket folder. Be sure to number each pot. Ask students to count the money in each pot. In the pocket folder can also be duplicated answer sheets (one for each student to complete) and a pencil. An answer key listing the total amount in each pot can also be provided to make this a self-checking activity.

Laminate each pot after the coins have been stamped. The entire activity can be stored in a small flat box.

Some pots of gold could be labeled with money story problems such as "How much money would be left in the pot if you spent one dollar?" Students would then write the amount of change on their answer sheets.

Super Thinker

Super Thinker is a game to play in math class. It is nice way to provide a break in the routine. Simply say, "It's time to play Super Thinker." Then draw the outline of a head on the chalkboard.

Give students a series of numbers to add, subtract, multiply, or divide in their heads. Each student should write each answer on paper. Walk around the room and check the answers or call for hands of those who are correct as you write the answer on the board.

Next, write the names of the students who had the correct answer inside the head shape. Students enjoy this break, even those who find math difficult to deal with. It is a fun way to drill facts. If a student is correct more than once, place hash marks next to his or her name.

Make a String Graph

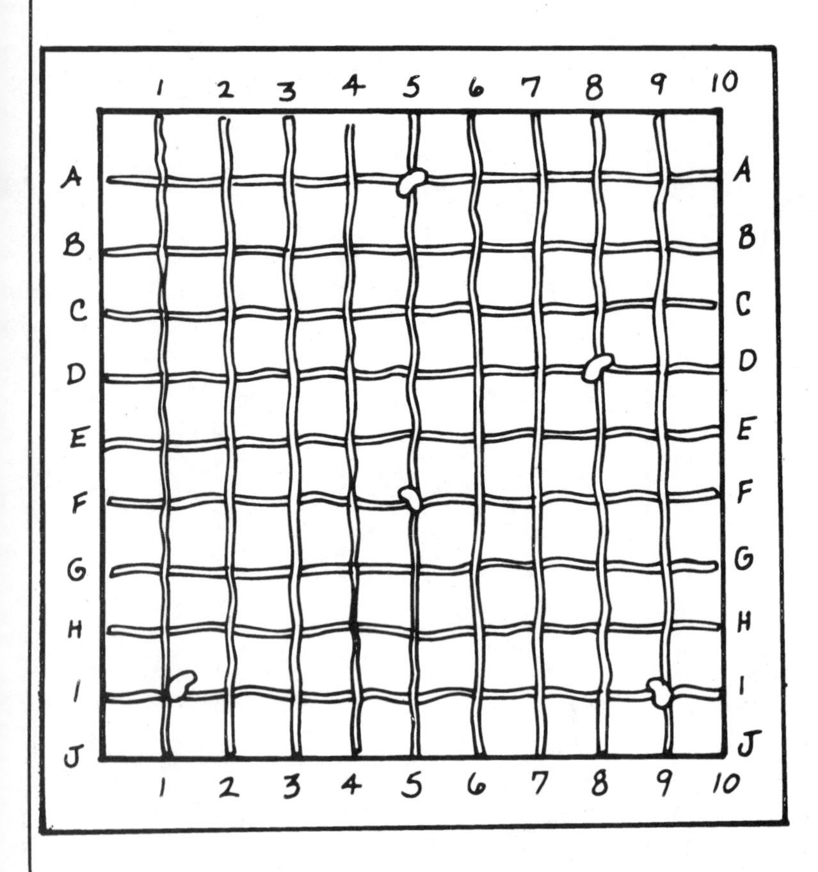

Materials

- construction paper
- string
- scissors
- ruler
- pencil
- beans (pinto, lima, and so on) or noodles

Made by Mary
A,5 D,8
F,5 I,1 I,9

Measure and draw lines that are 1" (2.5 cm) apart, vertically and horizontally on a blank piece of construcion paper. Make at least 10 lines each way. Choose letters and numbers, and label your grid vertically and horizontally.

Now cut string the length of your lines and glue it right on top of each line you drew.

Glue beans or noodles at various coordinates. Let them dry overnight. Display your finished map on the bulletin board. Make a label with your name and list the coordinates of your beans. Place the label next to your map.

Roll a Product

Each player will need a game board like the one illustrated. Create four dice from wooden cubes. Two should be numbered 0, 1, 2, 3, 4, and 5 with a blue marker. The other two cubes should be numbered 0, 6, 7, 8, 9, and 10 with a red marker. Provide dried beans or pennies to use as game markers.

To start, each player rolls a red die. The one with the largest number is the first player. In turn, the player selects and rolls two dice. The product of the two numbers shown on the top faces is covered on the game board. If the product is already covered, the player loses a chance to cover a square. Play continues in this manner until one player has six markers in a horizontal row or seven markers in a vertical row.

Roll a Product					
1	50	60	70	80	90
0	2	3	4	5	6
7	8	9	10	12	14
15	16	18	20	21	24
25	27	28	30	32	35
36	40	42	45	48	49
54	56	63	64	72	81

Pair Up for Math Fun

Let students pair off to solve problems in two-digit addition and subtraction. The first student adds or subtracts the ones column, the second student, the tens. Colored pencils make this activity more fun. Score a point for each example worked correctly. Which pair in the classroom can work most accurately? Expand this idea to include three- and four-digit numbers as well as multiplication and division.

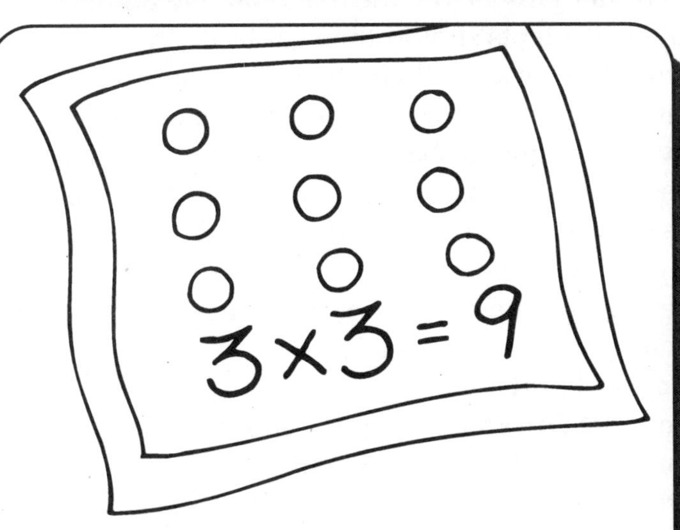

Wholly Number Facts

To illustrate a number fact, have each student write the fact on a piece of construction paper and use a paper punch to make holes to illustrate the fact. Mount the papers on a contrasting background. Display on a bulletin board, or punch a hole in each and tie with yarn for a booklet.

Times Champ

Make a game board like the one below. You will also need two sets of markers, each a different color. On each set of markers, write the products made by multiplying the numbers on the game board. The completed markers should be separated according to color. Each player receives a set.

Play begins with each pile of markers turned facedown. Each player, in turn, picks a marker, turns it over and reads the product. The player then places the marker on the playing board in the correct box. If the player cannot do this, the marker is set aside, and it is the next player's turn.

A player may challenge an opponent's placement. If the marker is in the wrong box, it must be removed and put on the bottom of the pile. It is the next player's turn. If the player was correct, the opponent loses his or her next turn.

The game stops when no more markers can be played. The winner is the person with the most markers on the board, or play for a specific amount of time.

X	1	2	3	4	5	6	7	8	9
1									
2									
3									
4									
5									
6									
7									
8									
9									

Ice Melt Mania

Your class will "warm up" to this icy estimating activity! Prepare a tray of ice cubes tinted with blue food coloring. Provide each team of students with a small, clear glass jar or bowl; a spoon; and a stopwatch. Challenge each group to estimate the number of minutes or seconds that it will take for a blue ice cube to melt when placed in a jar or bowl containing hot water. Invite groups to write their estimates on a piece of paper. Fill each jar or bowl with hot water before dropping a blue ice cube into it. Have one student in each group use the stopwatch to measure the passing time. Students may stir the water with the spoon to speed up the melting process, or just sit and watch as the cube dissolves. Instruct students to press STOP on their stopwatches when the cube has completely melted. Help teams to find the difference between their estimates and the actual melting times. List the differences on a chart. Identify the three smallest differences. Discuss which teams used their spoons. Award the appropriate number of snowballs (marshmallows) to each winning team.

Scoring Points

Smallest Difference—first: 3 snowballs; second: 2 snowballs; third: 1 snowball

The Great Snowball Grab

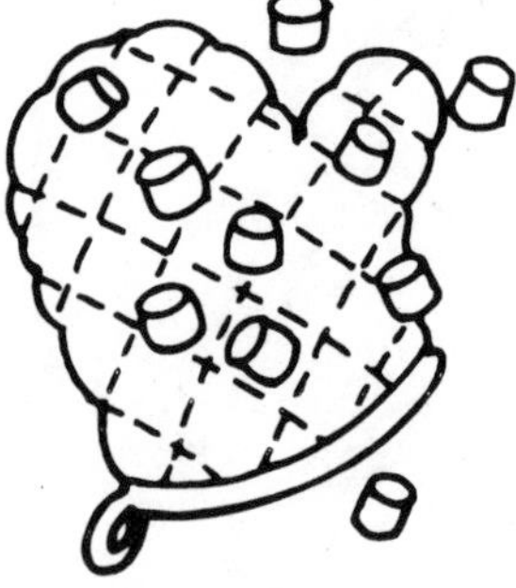

A large bowl of mini marshmallows and a thick, colorful mitten are all you'll need for this exciting estimating activity! Provide each student with a 5" x 5" (13 x 13 cm) piece of paper, split by a diagonal line. Challenge students to estimate the number of "snowballs" (mini marshmallows) that they will be able to grab while wearing the mitten. Ask students to write their estimates above the diagonal line on their pages. The fun begins as each student steps forward, puts on the mitten, reaches into the bowl, and grabs as many snowballs as possible. Only one grab is permitted. The competitors must have a firm hold on their snowballs before being allowed to drop the handfuls onto paper plates set beside the bowl. As a class, count each plate of snowballs, then have each student record his or her tally below the diagonal line on the paper. Students should then calculate the difference between their estimates and the actual number of snowballs grabbed from the bowl. Invite students to share their answers. Identify the three students with the smallest differences. Also recognize the three students who were able to grab the greatest number of snowballs. Award the appropriate number of snowballs (marshmallows) to each team.

Scoring Points

Smallest Difference—first: 3 snowballs; second: 2 snowballs; third: 1 snowball

Greatest Grab—first: 3 snowballs; second: 2 snowballs; third: 1 snowball

Snow Shoveling Estimation

Snow removal has never been so much fun! Display three large, clear glass jars in a variety of sizes and shapes. Fill each jar with "snow" (flour). Pass several "snow shovels" (teaspoons) around the classroom for students to examine. Challenge students to estimate the number of "shovels" full of "snow" in each of the three jars. After the estimates have been recorded on paper, invite the class to help with the shoveling. Encourage students to think of timesaving methods that may be used to measure the amount of snow in the jars. Discuss each suggestion. Be sure to have a set of measuring cups standing by. One clever snow shoveler is sure to suggest identifying the number of teaspoons in one cup and then using the cup to remove and measure the snow. Work together to empty the snow from jars 1, 2, and 3. Ask the class to identify the difference between their three estimates and the actual number of shovels in each jar. Identify the three students who had the smallest differences for each jar. Award the appropriate number of snowballs (marshmallows) to each team.

Scoring Points

Smallest Difference—Jar 1: first: 3 snowballs; second: 2 snowballs; third: 1 snowball. **Jar 2:** first: 3 snowballs; second: 2 snowballs; third: 1 snowball. **Jar 3:** first: 3 snowballs; second: 2 snowballs; third: 1 snowball

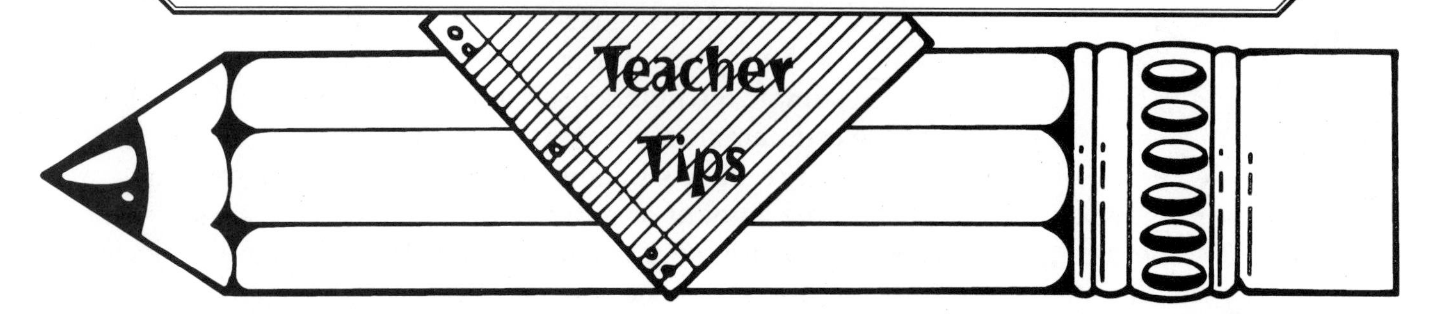

Fun With Ice Cubes

- Let students try all sorts of ways to get an ice cube to melt. No hot water allowed! Try radiators, fans, crushing, and so on. Each student will think of plenty of ways to make his or her ice cube melt the fastest.
- Then have a contest to determine who can keep an ice cube frozen the longest. No refrigerators or freezers allowed! Supply newspapers, sandwich bags, foil, boxes, cotton, and so on. Set a time limit, possibly overnight, to see whose cube remains the largest.
- Try putting different things on an ice cube: a penny, a washer, thumbtacks, wood, chalk, a ring, salt, paper, a paper clip.
- Float ice cubes in water, oil, salt water, or alcohol. What happens? Does an ice cube melt faster than a snowball? Color some ice cubes yellow, some red, some blue. Serve them in pairs in lemonade. What happens? This is a nice thing to do at a party during the winter season.
- Older students should study the Ice Age. Find out what a glacier is. How was it formed? Where are glaciers found today?
- Provide containers in a variety of sizes and shapes in which you can freeze water. Use these containers to make funny-shaped ice cubes. Which cubes melt the fastest? Time the melting process.
- Bring a snowball in from outside. Put it in a dish. Have students write down what time it is and how long they think it will take the snowball to melt. Each student then figures how many minutes "off" he or she was.
- Bring some snow into the classroom. Put it in several dishes of different sizes. Cover some dishes with paper and others with leaves. Sand, salt, rocks, cloth, and soil can also be used. Which dish of snow melts the fastest? Why?

Experimenting With Prisms

Problem—How can liquids act as a prism?

Materials
- a light source (flashlight, film projector)
- bowl/small pan
- pocket mirror

Procedure

Discuss with students the colors of the rainbow and the spectrum formed when light passes through a prism. Explain that if water takes a triangular shape, it may act as a prism and break light into its component colors.

Next, give each group a pan or bowl of water, a light source, and a mirror (preferably about 2" x 3" [5 x 8 cm]). Instruct students to attempt to arrange the materials so that a spectrum is formed. Darken the room so that if spectra are reflected on the wall or ceiling, they will be seen more easily.

If no students discover the right solution, instruct them as follows: Place the mirror in the pan or bowl of water so that one end rests on the edge and the other is on the bottom. Be sure not to proceed until the water has settled because rippling water will not work. When a mirror is angled through the water in this way, a triangular area of water is created. Now, shine the light source at about a 45^{0} angle toward the mirror. Try various angles. A spectrum will be reflected by the mirror on the wall or ceiling. Have some students try this using glycerine or mineral oil as liquids in place of water.

This experiment shows how water may act as a prism and also provides students with an opportunity to manipulate materials and make observations.

Sponge Garden

The following idea can be used in conjunction with science units dealing with plants and seeds. It's fun for students to see how different seeds look as they grow.

Soak a sponge and put it in a dish of water. Sprinkle seeds over the top of the sponge. Try different kinds of seeds, which might be left over from planting a garden. Grass seeds and birdseed also work well.

Keep water in the dish so the sponge doesn't dry out. When leaves appear, you'll know that the food stored in the seeds is used up. Add liquid plant food to the water to keep your plants healthy.

Watch your sponge garden. You'll be surprised how tall it grows!

Weather Art

This is a fun way to work in art with your daily weather forecasts. Select one student to be the artist who will serve for a week at a time. Portion a part of your bulletin board for weather forecasts. The student or students responsible for posting the weather report for the day places their notice on the bulletin board. The artist for the week reads the report and sketches a scene to illustrate the prediction: a rainy scene on a rainy day, a sunshiny scene on a sunshiny day, a snowy scene when it snows, and so on. The scene is placed under or beside the forecast on the bulletin board. Change artists and weather reporters after they have served for a week to allow others to participate. If space allows, you may leave the daily forecasts and illustrations up for the entire week so that all students will have sufficient time to read and reread the bulletins and enjoy the art.

Through this activity, students become more proficient in reading weather words. They begin to understand the use of degrees; wind velocity and direction; what highs and lows are; cold fronts; symbols used by weather forecasters for rain, snow, air flow, and so on. They get to know the use of the word *percent,* and concepts such as *light and variable.*

Newspaper weather reports will probably be used more by students than the TV reports as it is easier to clip the newspaper bulletin than it is to jot down what the TV reporter says. However, both will be used from time to time.

Shadow Clock

Explain to students that they can use shadows to help tell time.

Tape a sheet of white paper to a piece of heavy cardboard. Stick a nail through the center of the paper and cardboard leaving most of the nail showing.

Have students go outside early on a sunny day and find a flat spot to lay the cardboard. Use a few small rocks to hold the cardboard in place.

Start marking the shadow of the nail on the paper with a pencil. Every hour or so mark, where the shadow is on the paper. Be sure to write the time above the mark.

The next day, have students check their shadow clocks to see if they tell the right time.

Discuss whether or not the clocks would tell the right time if someone moved the cardboard. Do students think the clocks will be right on time a week later? A month later? All year long?

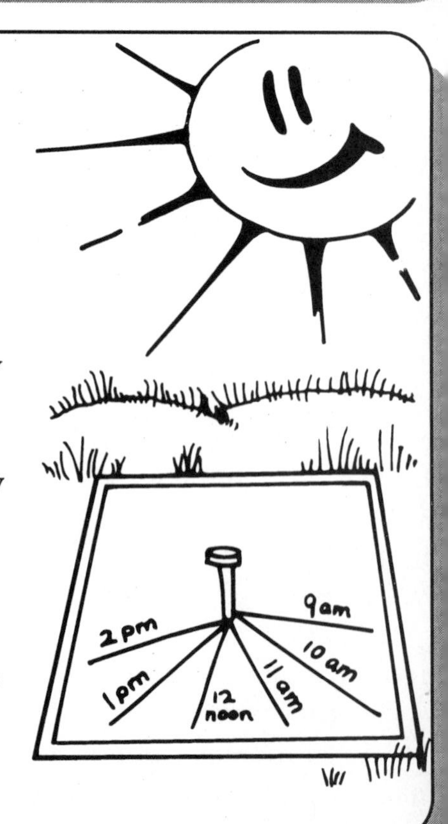

Invite ROY G. BIV to Your Classroom

Why not invite Roy G. Biv to your classroom for a science and art lesson? His initial appearance might be via a prism or a simple chandelier crystal catching the sunlight through the window. Students can make observations about the rainbow patterns made by the prism.

Have each student take out his or her crayons and locate red, orange, yellow, green, blue, indigo, and violet. On a large sheet of butcher paper, each student or group can design the following character: Mr. Roy G. Biv has a red ball on his orange hat and a yellow face with a green beard. He has a blue shirt and mittens, indigo pants, and violet boots.

Younger children may enjoy coloring an outline drawing of Mr. Biv.

Have students research why the colors of the rainbow are always in a particular order and what causes a rainbow, a double rainbow, and so on. Students can write poems, myths, or legends about rainbows and their origins.

Students can make small line drawings of themselves or Mr. Biv and then lightly write their names in cursive so that each figure is holding the name, like a jump rope or a lasso. Using seven strands of bright yarn, glue them on in the correct rainbow order so that the name is seven strands wide.

Poor Richard

Introduce the almanac to the class. Explain how many people use the phases of the moon to determine when to plant crops. Provide shapes of the moon's phases to attach to the classroom calendar each day.

Home Sweet Moon

It is the year 2050. Living space on Earth has become scarce. Plans are made to colonize the moon. What elements would be necessary for human survival on the moon? Describe the facility you would build for the colonists.

Dancing Germs

Find pictures of bacteria and viruses in encyclopedias. Provide students with a variety of materials for creating imaginary germs. These might include: yarn, toilet tissue cores, chenille stems, and 1 1/4" (3 cm) and 1/4" (.6 cm) gummed circles. You will also need large needles, medium needles, and black thread. Some ideas are shown here. Your students will probably have many more.

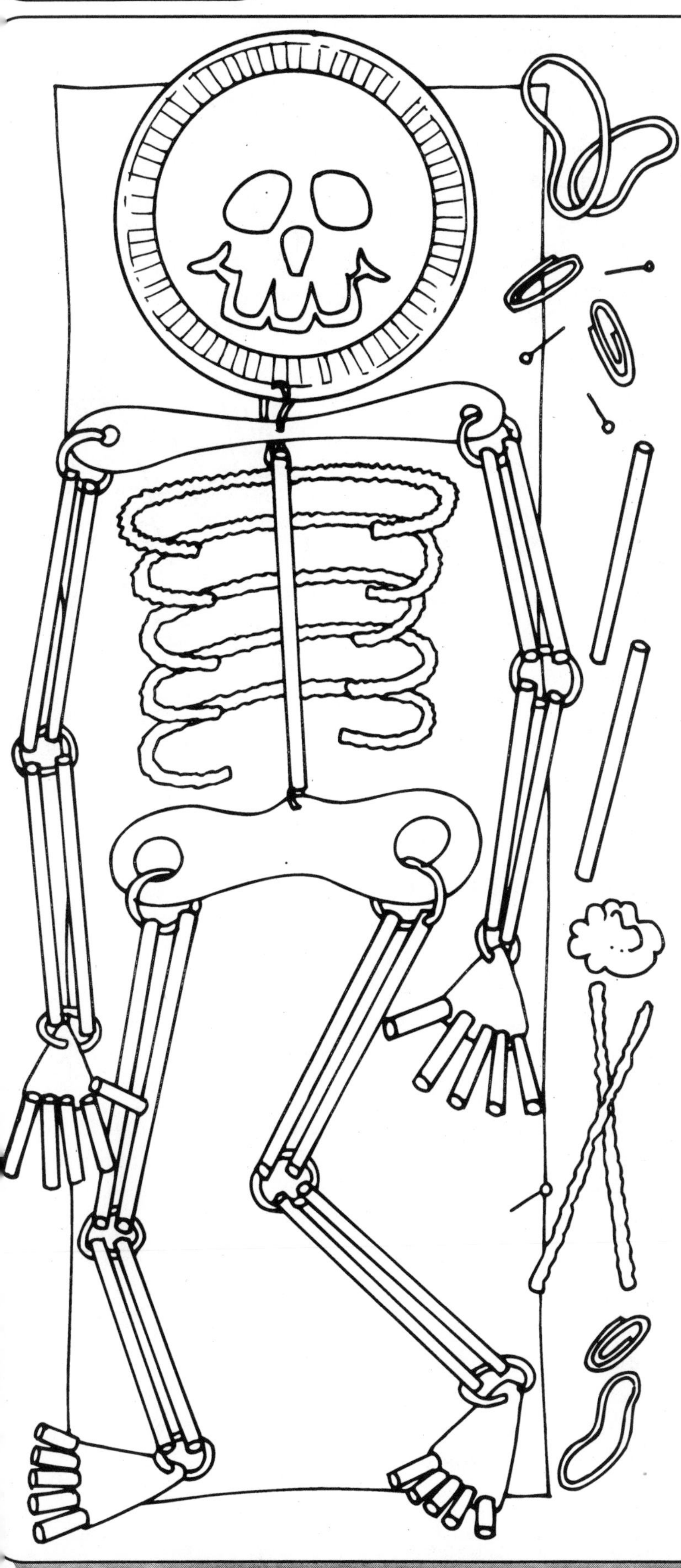

The First Annual Awesome Skeleton-Building Contest

The First Annual Awesome Skeleton Building Contest can be used to top off a unit on the skeletal system. Each student is provided with the following materials:

- 1 paper plate
- 1 blob of white clay
- 10 rubber bands
- 14 plastic straws
- 1 piece of white paper
- 4 paper clips
- 14 pipe cleaners
- 10 straight pins

Have scissors, tape, and glue available to everyone. The time limit is one hour.

Objective: Build a model human skeleton, standing or hanging.

Rules: Use only the materials you have. You do not have to use all the materials, but leftovers must be put away in their original containers.

Awards: Skeleton stickers on note cards with the following captions can be presented:

First One Done
Tallest
Shortest
Most Realistic
Sturdiest Rib Cage
You choose criteria

What a variety of skeletons can be created! The hour passes quickly with not a sound coming from the young scientists. Completed skeletons can be displayed against a black paper background.

The Bug Jar Trivia Game

Send your students on an insect trivia hunt to help make a class trivia game. They may use encyclopedias and other reference books to research their information.

Divide your class into small teams and ask each team to write questions (with answers) on 3" x 5" (8 x 13 cm) cards on their assigned subject. Some suggested categories are: ants, butterflies, bees, crickets, grasshoppers, flies, and beetles. Have a brainstorming session with your class to add more to the list.

Put the completed trivia question cards in a large glass jar labeled **The Bug Jar** and play a round or two during those extra minutes of the day!

To further extend this activity, teachers may want to have each trivia team write a mini report on its assigned insect to be presented to the class. Some suggestions are: making poster reports (with pictures and facts), creating a television game show or news program that features their insect facts, and an imaginary interview with an entomologist.

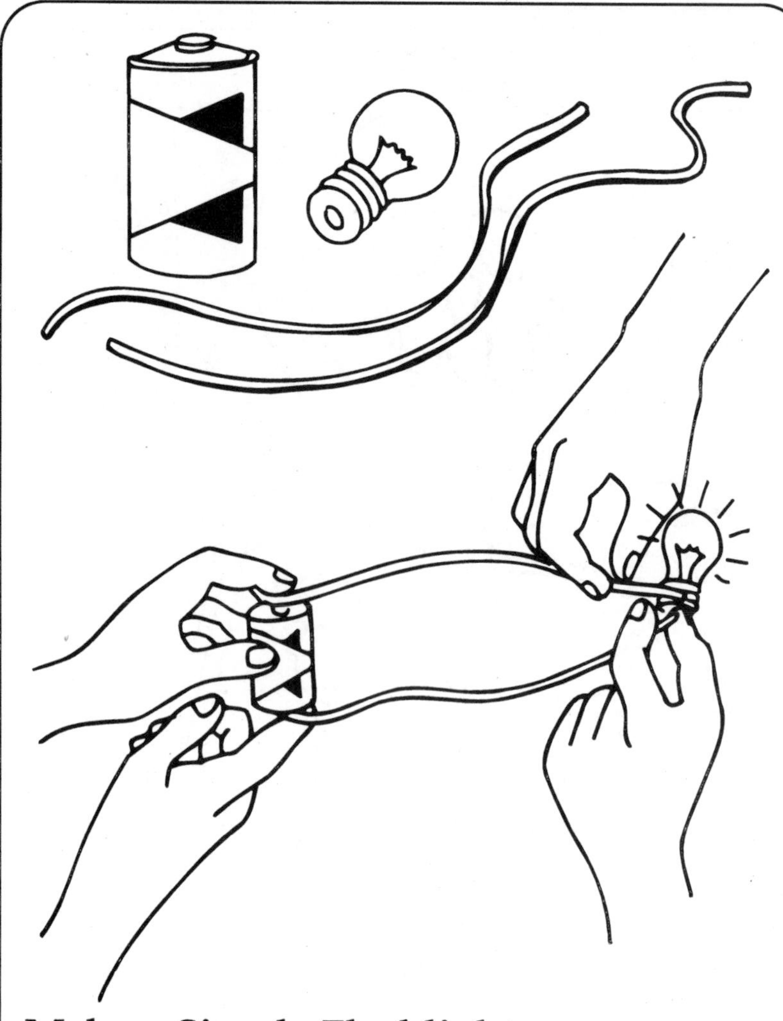

Make a Simple Flashlight

Materials

- 1 flashlight battery cell (size C or D)
- 1 flashlight bulb for a 1- or 2-cell flashlight
- 2 copper wires (14 to 20 gauge)

Student Instructions

With a partner, have your helper hold the cell in his or her hands and press one end of each wire against *each* terminal of the cell (bottom and center terminals). Hold the bulb down on a wooden tabletop and place the loose end of *one* wire against the metal side of the bulb.

Place the loose end of the *other* wire on the center connection of the bulb bottom. The bulb should light. **Note:** A serviceable light can be made by soldering the connections at battery and bulb and inserting a small switch in one of the wires.

Seek and Find—Then Classify

Ask your class to collect a variety of rocks, looking for different colors, sizes, shapes, and textures. If you do not live in an area where a field trip is convenient, it works just as well to use a rock collection from a local library or your school's library.

Once you have your rocks, you are set to go! Divide the class into groups of three or four. Ask students to make separate piles of their rocks according to color, size, shape, texture, and luster. Encourage them to think up their own ideas for other categories.

To enhance math skills, chart results by listing the number of rocks that fit into each category.

Nests, Insects, Rocks, and Shells

Spark your students' enthusiasm for science by creating your own classroom science museum. You can transform an area with empty shelves into one of the most popular spots at school! Here's how to create your museum.

1. Have a brainstorming session with your class and talk about your plans to have a museum.
2. Have students vote on a name for your museum. With students' help, decide on the categories of items you would like to display in your museum. Some suggestions are: shells, rocks, nests, insects, seeds, leaves and bark, ocean creatures (dried starfish, seahorses), and so on.
3. Make bright, laminated signs to label each shelf with its category. Line your shelves with colorful construction paper. You may want to set up a microscope mini center nearby to enable students to take a closer look at some of the museum items, such as leaves and seeds.
4. When the museum is ready, encourage students to bring in items to share with the class. Have them label each item with their name for easy identification.

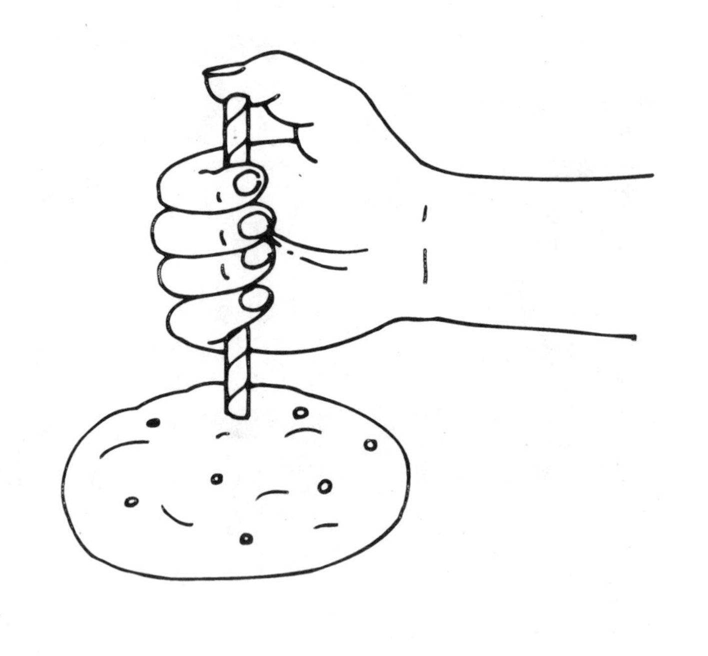

The Straw Plunger

1. **Materials:** one firm raw potato and one plastic drinking straw per person
2. **Procedure:** Cover one end of the straw with your thumb. Plunge the straw straight down into the potato. You may need to try several times to get the right angle and force.
3. Carefully remove the straw and see what, if anything, is in the straw. Why and how did this work?

Electrically Charged Straws

1. **Materials:** a small hill of salt and pepper and one drinking straw per person
2. **Procedure:** Rub a straw against dry hair or wool clothing. Will the straw stick to anything? What? If it can stick, why is it possible?
3. Now rub the straw again and hold it over the hill of salt and pepper. What happens? Was the salt and pepper attracted to the straw? Why or why not?

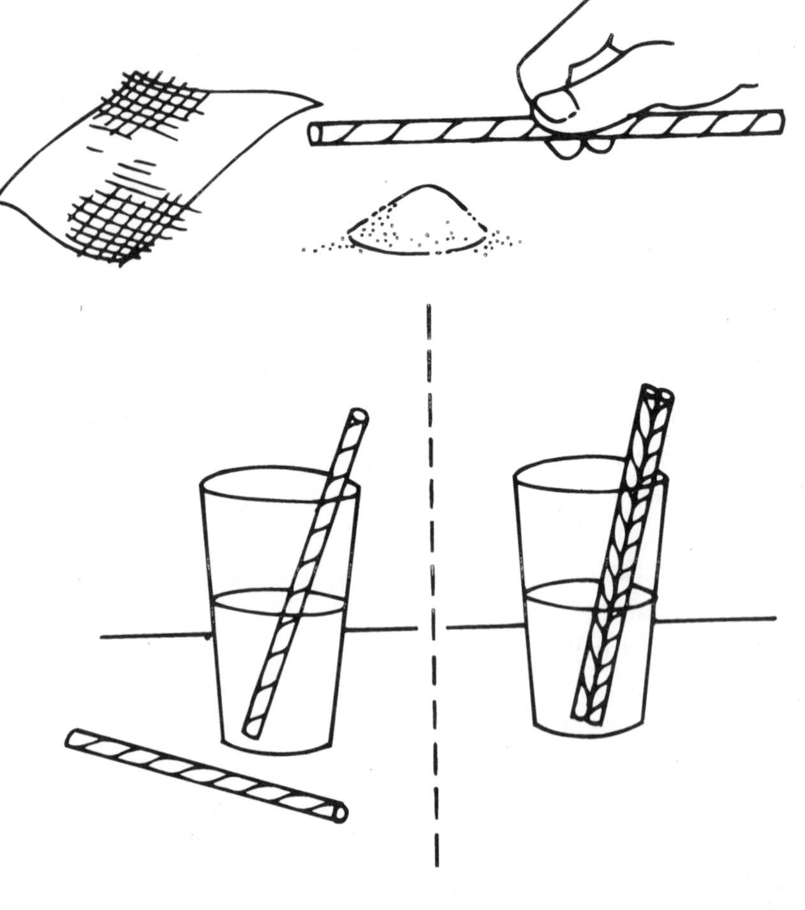

The Straw Elevator

1. **Materials:** two drinking straws per person; a colored beverage; and one clear glass per person, partially filled with the colored drink
2. **Procedure:** Place one straw in a glass of the colored beverage. Sip on the straw. Is it easy to drink? How does it work?
3. Place the second straw in the glass of drink and sip again. Will you get more to drink by using two straws rather than one? Why?

A Spider Is Watching

Instead of the usual classroom observation of a spider, reverse the situation: invite a spider to observe the classroom.

For a spider's-eye view of your world, you will need a gallon-sized glass jar. Add two cups of sand or soil and a bit of moss. A couple of twigs with leaves attached will support a web, plus provide a nook for hiding. Fill a bottle cap with water for thirsty inhabitants. Secure a piece of cheesecloth or netting over the top with a rubber band. Now, your habitat is ready for its first occupant. Locate a garden spider or another web-builder. With a stick, carefully place the spider in a small container. Transfer to the terrarium. Encourage students to observe and record data, using these questions:

1. What type of web is the spider building?
2. What are its favorite insects? (Place a fly, grasshopper, or others inside.)
3. When is the spider most active?

Return the spider to the outside in a few days and replace with another species. Compare the two spiders.

Salt and Ice

How does salt affect water's ability to freeze?

Materials

- 1 ice-cube tray
- water
- measuring spoons
- tablespoon
- table salt

Procedure

1. Fill each of the spaces in the ice-cube tray with 1 tablespoon (15 ml) of water.
2. Leave plain water in two of the spaces.
3. Add 1/8 teaspoon (.625 ml) salt to each of the next two spaces.
4. Add 1/4 teaspoon (1.25 ml) salt to the next two spaces.
5. Continue adding an extra 1/8 teaspoon (.625 ml) salt every two spaces until all the spaces are filled.
6. Put the tray in the freezer.
7. After about two hours, check the ice-cube tray. What observations can students make? What is their conclusion about how salt affects the freezing of water?

Ice Balls

In the dead of winter, take advantage of the freezing temperatures for this science lesson. Give each of your students a balloon. Allow students to fill their balloons with water. These balloons belong to each student, and students need to watch them carefully and record their behavior.

Take the water balloons outside. Find a new outdoor home for each balloon and leave it there until it is frozen solid. Check the water in the balloons after four or five hours. When the liquid (water) turns to a solid (ice), bring the balloons back into the classroom and place in buckets, coffee cans, or other waterproof containers. Observe the ice balls and record data on the form below. Make individual comparisons and classroom comparisons.

Record the outdoor temperature and indoor temperature. ___________

Ice Ball Chart

1. What shape is your ice ball? _________
2. Would you say it is small, medium, or large?_________
3. How many hours did it take the water in your balloon to freeze? _________
4. What form of water did you put in the balloon? _________
5. What form is in it now? _________

   Peel back the balloon and remove the ice ball.
6. Measure your ice ball. length _________ width _________
7. Record the melting process. Make a chart and record the size and amount of water each hour or each day in the container.
8. How long did it take for your ice ball to melt completely? _________
9. How much water is in your container? _________
10. How long will it take to refreeze this water? _________
11. How long will it take to thaw the ice? _________

Bulletin Boards

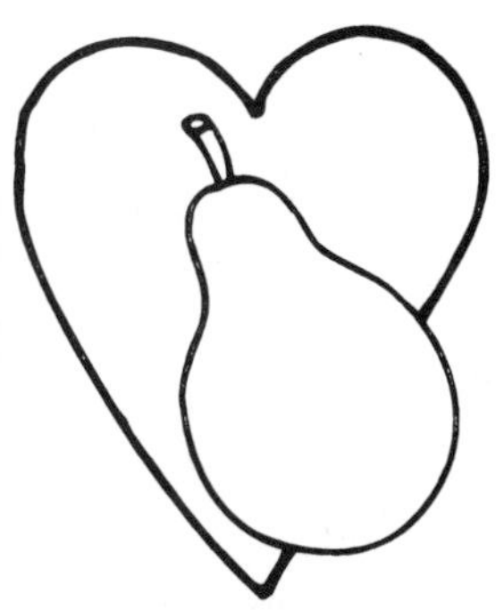

Couples by the Pair

This is a great idea for Valentine's Day or anytime. Draw a large pear and place it on a bulletin board. Title the board "Couples by the Pair." Students then write names of famous couples inside the pear. Let them write as many as they can think of. Then have each student choose one couple and write a paragraph explaining why that couple was or is famous.

Bulletin Board Borders

Patterns can be purchased for making different shapes of borders, or you can make your own by cutting zigzag or curvy lines or by using pinking shears.

Bulletin Borders

Cut out 2" (5 cm) strips of brightly colored paper to be used as a bulletin board border. Instead of leaving it plain, give each student a section of the border. Then have him or her decorate the section according to the season or theme needed or just with a pleasant design.

Use this artwork as the border to decorate your room. Students will love seeing their own work used to finish off the bulletin boards.

A Winter's Night

Create your own fun and easy bulletin board winter scene. Students will also enjoy creating a small-scale picture of their very own.

Materials

- black posterboard or construction paper
- white cutouts of snowy hills, houses, trees, stars, sleds, rooftops, and hanging icicles
- Santa and reindeer (optional)
- masking tape
- glue

Directions

1. Cover the work table with newspaper for easy cleanup.
2. Mount black posterboard to bulletin board.
3. Attach white cutouts as desired to construct your winter scene. Students should glue cutouts to black paper.
4. Hang students' winter scenes on the wall for a spectacular effect. Enjoy the wonderful scenes you have created.

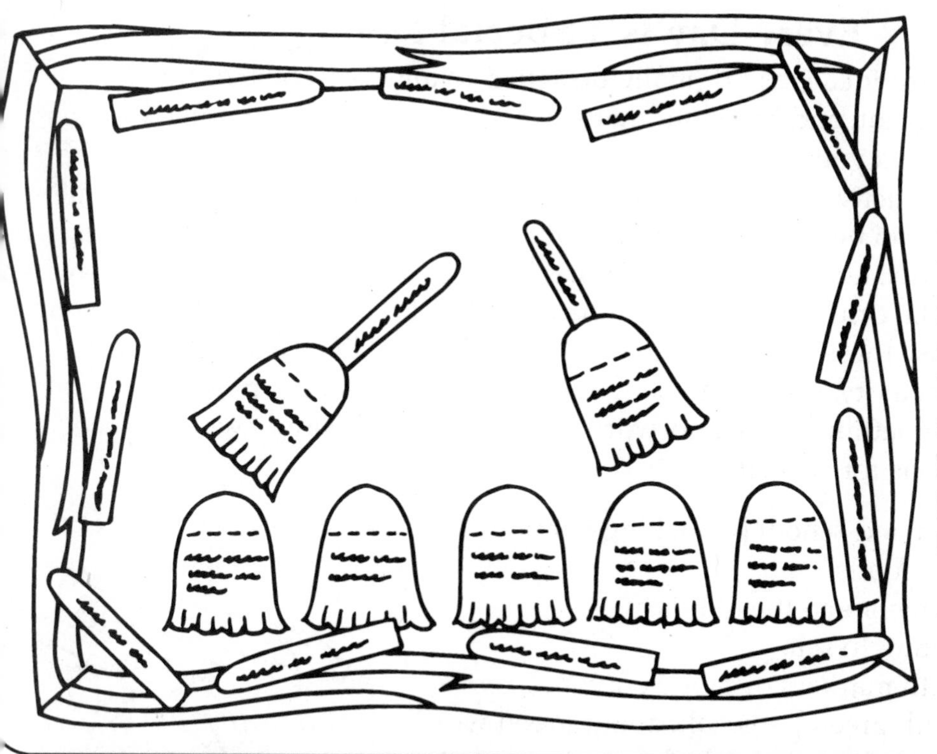

Make a Clean Sweep!

Make brooms and handles from construction paper and laminate after skills have been printed on them with a felt-tip pen. You may wish to save time by drawing broom and handle patterns on a master and duplicating the number of copies needed. Label a bulletin board area "Make a Clean Sweep!" Place the broom handles around the bulletin board. The brooms can be tacked across the bottom for students to match.

A Class License

For a unique welcome-back-to-school display, make a license plate for each student and arrange them on a wall, door, or bulletin board.

Make a license plate for each student on different-colored posterboard. Cut students' names, name of the school, state, and school years from construction paper. Glue on the license plates. Laminate. Make a display using an appropriate caption such as *Licensed for Fourth Grade*. The plates can later be put on the front of pupils' desks for name plates.

When class pictures are taken, make each child a "learning permit" patterned after your states' drivers' licenses. Paste the picture in the upper left-hand corner. Laminate the permits and use in conjunction with a class discipline policy. If a student is caught disobeying a rule, the learning permit is taken away for a certain amount of days, depending on the infraction.

At the end of the year, the license plates and permits are given to students to take home.

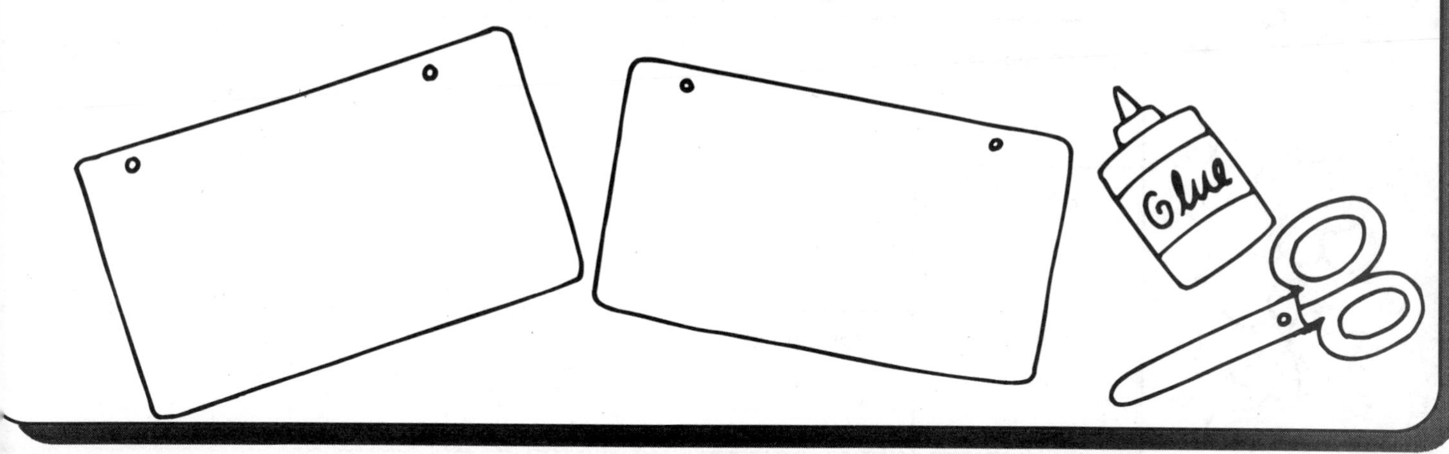

Every Day Is a Special Day

This bulletin board idea was originally designed to alleviate some of the restlessness, excitement, and boredom that surfaces at the end of the year. Together, plan the kinds of days your class is interested in, and then put a schedule together. (Individual or daily activities were not listed so that there was always an element of surprise.) There can be a lot of creative writing with this activity—paragraphs, stories, posters, cards, letters, and much more. You can include parties, crazy days, read-a-thons, and favorite days. Each day has a word of the day so that at least one new word will be learned each day. Use these words as much as possible—students will be thrilled with their new vocabulary. With this activity, you can make your last month of school much more exciting for students and give them something to look forward to. What a great way to wrap up the school year! Below is a list of a few ideas for special days.

Hometown Day—Celebrate your town and school by making banners, buttons, posters, and maps.
Tasting Party—Taste new and unusual foods.
Old-Fashioned Day—Dress up like someone in the old days.
Rummage Sale Day—Dredge up old junk to sell.
T-Shirt Day—Decorate old T-shirts with markers or fabric crayons.
Green Day—Eat green foods, write with green pens, talk about green words, wear green.
Book Character Day—Dress up like your favorite book character.

Every Day Is a Special Day

Monday	Tuesday	Wednesday	Thursday	Friday
T-Shirt Day Decorate a T-shirt.	Popcorn Day	Rummage Sale Day	Art Day	Favorite State Day
Favorite Person Day	Favorite Animal Day	Wildlife Day	Dress-Up-Like-a-Book-Character Day	Safety Day
Surprise Day	Dad's Day	Field Trip Day	Ecology Day	Pet Day
Career Day	Read-a-thon Day	Old-Fashioned Day	Tasting Party Day	Track Meet Day
Mom's Day	Green Day	Plant-a-Flower Day	Favorite Country Day	Day Off

A Valentine Bulletin Board

Brighten your classroom with this delightful bulletin board idea.

Materials
- pink and red construction paper
- white posterboard
- glue
- small white doilies

Directions
1. Cut out two large hearts from white posterboard. Glue pointed tips together to form a body.
2. Cut out four small hearts from white posterboard for hands and feet.
3. Cut two short red strips for arms and two long red strips for legs.
4. Glue arms and legs to lower body heart.
5. Glue small white hearts to red strips for hands and feet.
6. Fashion a perky red hat and add colorful hearts as a decoration.
7. Use tiny self-stick hearts for facial features.

How to Create a Bulletin Board
1. Staple or tape pink construction paper to bulletin board. Place heart people where desired. Cut out two attached white hearts and print *Love Comes from the Heart* on them. Add these to the bulletin board.
2. Cut paper doilies in half and use as a border.

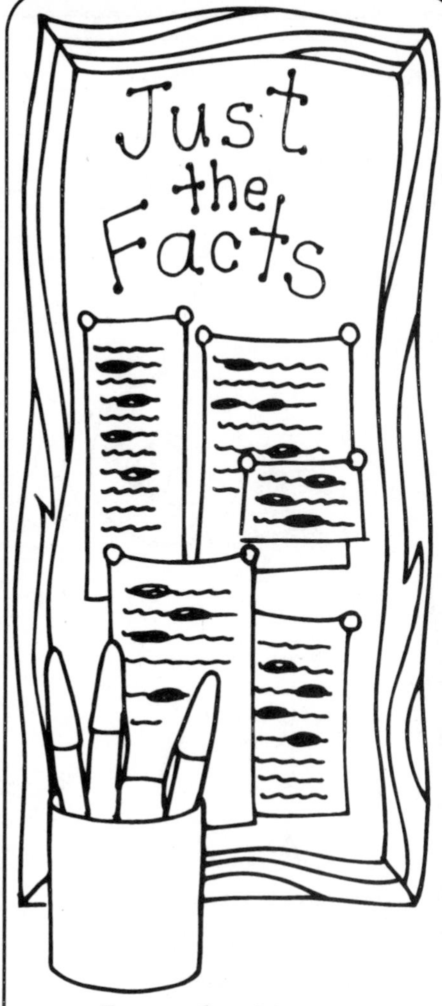

Just the Facts!

Give your students a chance to become real-word detectives or cub reporters while at the same time becoming familiar with proper nouns. Post numerous interesting newspaper articles around the bulletin board along with marking pens with three different colors of ink. Have students underline proper nouns with the appropriate color ink, using the categories of who, what, and where. Keep adding to the list on a notebook page, and change the news articles often. Students may also want to post their own articles.

Find the $1.00 Word

Make a chart similar to the one shown in the illustration. Place on a bulletin board along with a picture of a person dressed as a detective holding a magnifying glass.

Children pick any word and add up the numbers that stand for the letters in the word. Any word that equals $1.00 should be put on a card with the child's name and placed on the board.

Write On! . . . Munchies!

Find large pictures of foods students like to eat. Sometimes fast-food restaurants might be willing to share a few they use to advertise in their restaurants. Place the pictures on the bulletin board in a pleasing arrangement. Next to each munchy, place a sheet of heavy paper or tagboard with the name of the munchy written on it. (Tagboard is best for protecting the surface of the bulletin board.)

To use this bulletin board activity, students write on the tagboard. Students may simply list words that describe the munchies (*spicy, salty, cold*), write phrases describing the munchies (*smooth and cold, sliding down my throat*), or write poems or paragraphs about it (*Crispy, crunchy, fun to eat. My favorite munchies can't be beat.*). Encourage them to use their imaginations and to use words that appeal to the senses when they write.

Salty Cold Spicy Crunchy Crispy

Mr. Snowman

Create this snowman in your classroom to help motivate students and to reward good behavior.

Materials

- white posterboard
- felt scraps or buttons
- various other trimmings
- bags of cotton balls

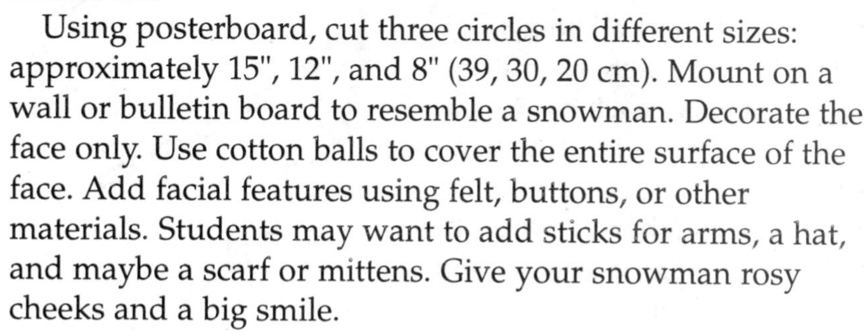

Directions

Using posterboard, cut three circles in different sizes: approximately 15", 12", and 8" (39, 30, 20 cm). Mount on a wall or bulletin board to resemble a snowman. Decorate the face only. Use cotton balls to cover the entire surface of the face. Add facial features using felt, buttons, or other materials. Students may want to add sticks for arms, a hat, and maybe a scarf or mittens. Give your snowman rosy cheeks and a big smile.

Procedure

After Mr. Snowman has been put together, explain that he will need more snow (cotton balls) to cover his body. The way to do this will be to earn a cotton ball and glue it to Mr. Snowman. Cotton balls may be awarded to individual students for good work or good behavior. Overall class behavior may also be rewarded at the end of each day.

When Mr. Snowman is completely covered, reward the class with a winter fun party, a movie, ice skating, and so on.

Making a Mr. Snowman to take home could also be part of the fun.

The Balloon Bunch

Here's a fun and attention-getting way to decorate a wall for open house or parents' night. Have each student print his or her name and carefully draw a self-portrait with markers on a balloon. Tie curly ribbon to each balloon and attach the balloons to the wall. Have the ribbons held by a student-drawn cartoon picture of the teacher. Caption above the balloons would read, *Mr. or Mrs. _____' Class.*

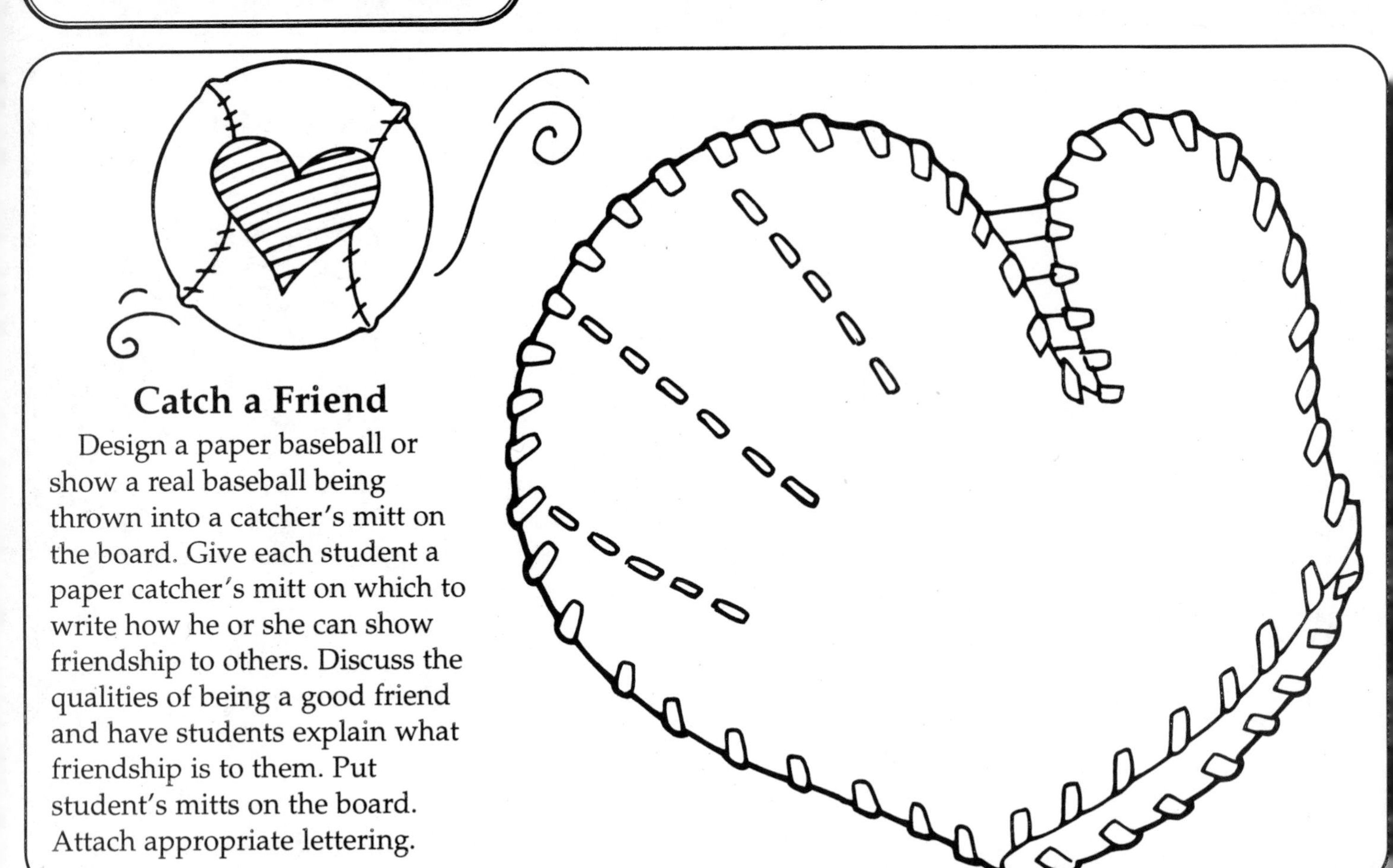

Catch a Friend

Design a paper baseball or show a real baseball being thrown into a catcher's mitt on the board. Give each student a paper catcher's mitt on which to write how he or she can show friendship to others. Discuss the qualities of being a good friend and have students explain what friendship is to them. Put student's mitts on the board. Attach appropriate lettering.

Cotton Candy for the Crowd

This activity can be used as a matching exercise or for individualizing assignments. Each cotton candy cone is made by rolling construction paper into a cone shape and stapling the back closed. Using flat rolled cotton, cut out puffy shapes for the cotton candy and fasten them to the bulletin board. "Snuggle" the cone shapes up under the edge of the cotton and fasten only the back to the bulletin board. Flatten them to form pockets to hold assignments written on 3" x 5" (8 x 13 cm) cards. Each student has his or her name on one of the cotton candy cones and a personalized assignment inside. To use the cotton candy for matching, place one word on each cone and the matching word or symbol on cards to be placed in the appropriate cone.

Patriotic Bulletin Boards

- "America the Beautiful"
- "My Country 'Tis of Thee"
- "So Proudly We Hail"
- "Let Freedom Ring"

Place letters across a large bulletin board announcing one of the above ideas. For "America the Beautiful," have children illustrate each phrase of the song with an appropriate picture. For example, *Oh beautiful for spacious skies,* could be illustrated in numerous ways, such as a sun and clouds; birds flying; planes and jets flying; or a night sky showing stars, moon, and constellations.

Another idea for illustrating the theme is to make a collage of pictures about our country, using either original drawings or pictures cut from magazines.

Seasonal

Embossed Eggs

You will need an 8 1/2" x 11" sheet of cardboard or posterboard as your base. Next, cut out egg shapes from heavy cardboard. Glue these randomly on your base. After the glue has dried, cover the entire surface with a sheet of aluminum foil. Glue or tape the edges of the foil to the back of the base. Now, with vivid-color crayons, color the foil to enhance the embossed areas.

Presidential Wax Museum

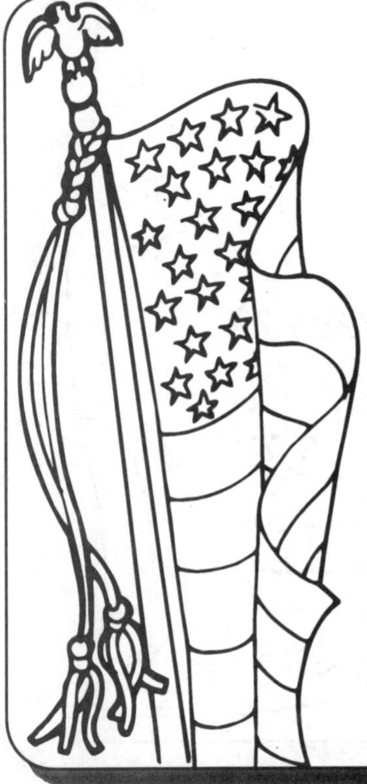

This is an activity that should be shared with other classes.

Assign a president to each student in the class. Students are to research the presidents and write a short speech about him, emphasizing interesting information that many may not know.

Also, thought should be given to clothes or physical features that make each president stand out (Washington—white powdered hair, cherry, hatchet; Carter—holding a bag of peanuts; Lincoln—hat and beard).

When all speeches have been written, have students memorize them. "Dress rehearsals" in costume will help them learn faster.

When you are satisfied that everyone is ready, schedule a Presidential Wax Museum Day. You (as narrator) introduce the president ("Our first president—George Washington") and shine a flashlight on that president. When the light is on the student, he or she should give the speech. The other presidents should remain still and "frozen" until it is their turn.

If possible, try to have someone film this so you can add this special activity to your class video library.

Hands-on Patriotism

Here is a project that can involve everyone in the school: students, teachers, janitors, the principal, cafeteria workers, and even bus drivers. Creating the American flag from paper hands can be a super patriotic effort for February—the birth month of two great presidents. Just have each person trace his or her hands and cut them out. A little planning will determine who should be red, white, blue, or black. Then have one student from each class outline his or her body, color it, and cut it out. Don't forget to include a couple of adults. These figures can be placed beneath the flag to represent those who worked on the project. Finally, find a large space near the entrance of the school or in the gym or cafeteria to tape up the flag. If the hands are glued on large strips of paper before being placed on the wall, the flag could be used for several years.

Glossy Eggs

Cut out large egg shapes from heavy white paper (something similar to watercolor paper). Open a can of condensed milk and pour into several containers. Add drops of food coloring to each to make lovely pastel paints. Using cotton swabs, paint Easter designs all over the paper eggs. Lay these flat to dry; they will take a couple of days to dry thoroughly. The smooth, glossy surface is surely worth the wait.

Paper Plate Presidents

Have each student make the face of a president on a paper plate, using the outer edge as the head. Make hair of yarn or cotton (wigs). Have students look at pictures of the presidents as they make their paper-plate presidents. Each student can make the president of his or her choice.

Uses

- Put the presidents up around the room in sequential order, with the dates of the presidencies below each.
- Put the presidents on tongue depressors and make puppets out of them.
- Have a puppet that is a reporter. Have the reporter interview the presidents to find out critical information about them, their presidencies, and the times.

The Real Meaning of *Love*

Valentine's Day is a fun holiday with thoughts of sweethearts and valentines filling our heads. Since love is the focus of the day, let students show love to someone in a special way.

1. Have each student bring in an old toy. Then have a Fix-Up-and-Repair Day. With a little cleaning, painting, and gluing, the toys will soon look like new. Donate these "new" toys to a children's hospital or orphanage.
2. Organize a We Can Help Make a Difference food drive involving the whole school. Place boxes around the building and encourage everyone to contribute a can of food. After the boxes are filled, have an organization pick them up.
3. Call your local humane society and arrange for a speaker to tell about unwanted and abused animals and what students can do to help these animals. Have students bring cans of pet food to be given to abused and unwanted animals at the animal shelter.

A Jar of Valentines

How about letting your students make no-calorie valentine candy jars to take home to friends and relatives? The jars of hearts can also be used as valentine cards.

The candy jars and valentines can be made from construction paper (any size you wish). Have each student fold a piece of white paper in half lengthwise and then draw half the jar on one side of the paper. Then cut out the jar and unfold it. Hearts can be cut out of red and pink construction paper. Each student can write personalized messages on the hearts for whomever is to receive the jar. Glue the completed hearts to the candy jar.

Variation

Cut two jars exactly the same size from waxed paper. Place the valentines on the waxy side of one of the jars and place the other waxed paper jar waxed-side down on top of the valentines. An adult or older student should then iron the jars together so that the two pieces of waxed paper stick together with the valentines between them.

Valentine Pals

As a special Valentine's Day classroom activity, use the pattern below to create simple Valentine Pals in which to hold student valentines. You will need the following.

- pink, red, and white felt squares
- red, yellow-orange, lime-green, and aqua yarn
- sticky craft glue
- polyester fiberfill (optional)

Fold a pink felt square in half and draw around the pattern, cutting out two bodies. Use white felt for hands, feet, and eyes; and red felt for the nose, heart, and eye centers. Mouths are created from red yarn; hair is made from the color yarn of your choice. Glue front side of body to its back side along the edges, leaving top of head unsealed to insert cards. Before glue dries, lift seams apart and insert tabs of hands and feet. Apply hair, facial features, and heart with glue.

When your pals have dried, they can hold valentine cards, and your students will have created a special Valentine's Day memento.

*If you do not wish to use this idea to make a card pouch, Valentine Pals may be stuffed with polyester fiberfill. Glue the edges around the head and you will have a clever valentine companion for each student.

Note: This pattern may be enlarged to fit your individual needs.

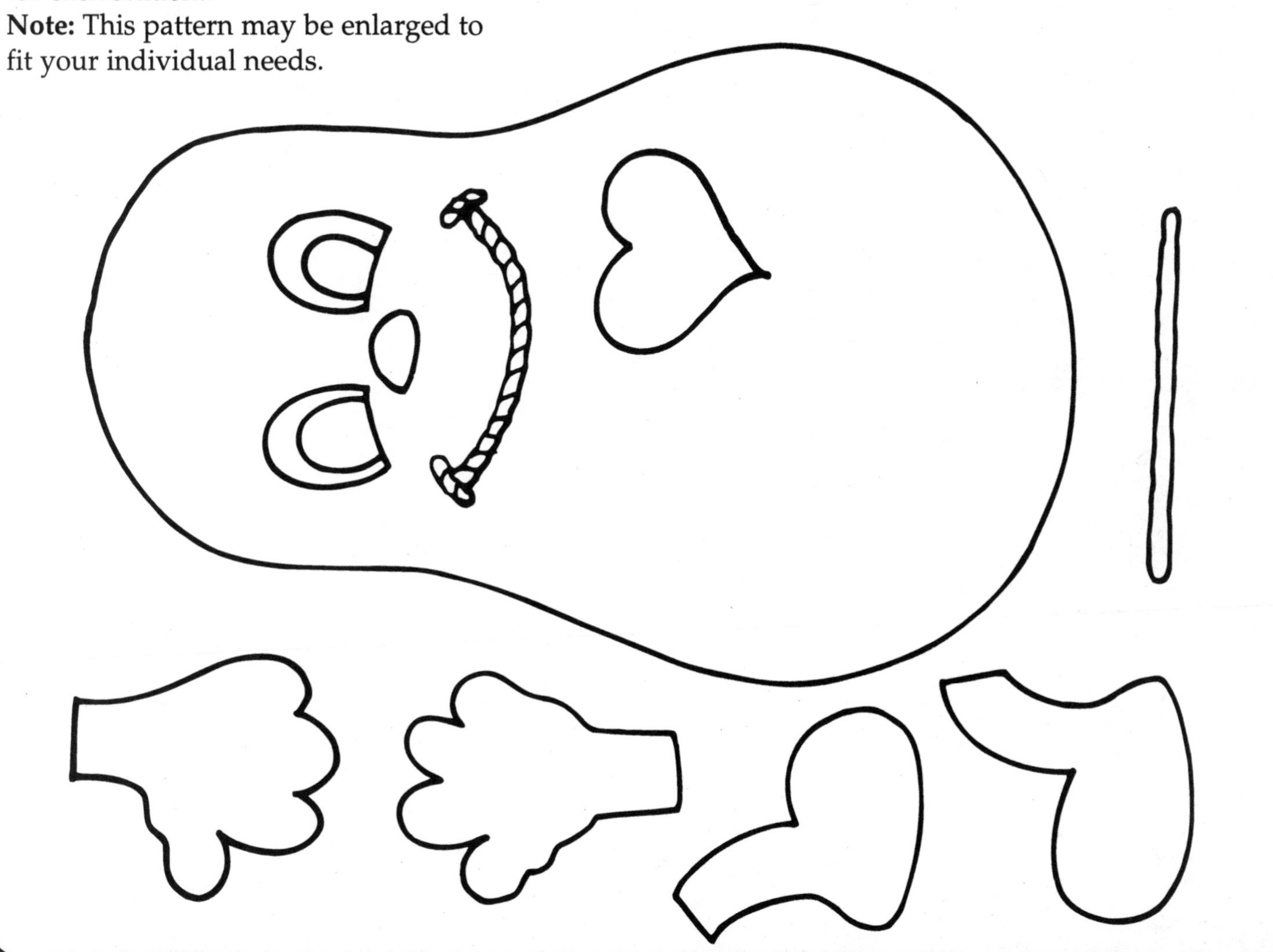

Valentines With Pictures

To create extra-special valentines, have students bring in magazines, catalogs, old calendars, or a personal photograph book. Let each student find a picture that appeals to him or her and write a jingle about it. To get creative juices flowing, have students make up some jingles for objects from the classroom. Have students cut out the pictures of their choice and glue them to cards made from construction paper. They should then write their jingles on the cards. See the following examples:

Ball: Let's have a ball, Valentine!
Record: I'm going on record to tell you I'm your Valentine.
Book: I'd like to book some time with you, Sweetheart.
Ring: Give me a ring sometime, Sweetie Pie.
Can: You can come to see me sometime, my dear.
Stamp: I can't stamp out my love for you.
Umbrella: I'd like to shower you with kisses.

A Leprechaun Booklet

Give an oval-shaped piece of white paper to each student. Ask him or her to draw and color a leprechaun on the paper. The leprechaun can be any size or doing anything the student wishes. Encourage creativity by using an example like a leprechaun crawling over a rainbow to get to a pot of gold.

Each student then writes a story or paragraph about the leprechaun he or she has drawn, complete with an appropriate title.

Collect the pictures and glue them into a booklet. Have students illustrate front and back covers for the booklet. Then photocopy a second booklet of the stories and pictures. Students will enjoy trying to match the stories with the pictures.

Students can make this activity even more special by presenting both booklets to younger children in the hospital.

Autumn Leaves

Each student draws a funny face on yellow, red, and orange paper leaves. The leaves are all put into a paper bag. Two teams play the game, the September Team and the October Team. The red leaves score 10 points; the yellow leaves score 4 points; the orange leaves score no points.

One student at a time, on alternating teams, takes one leaf from the bag and holds on to it. The teams continue to take turns until all the leaves have been taken from the bag. Then add up the scores for the leaves the students hold. The highest team score wins. The winning team cuts out a brown paper tree and tapes it to the wall. The top of the tree has a blank area for students to glue on their leaves. When the funny face leaves are glued in place, the personality tree becomes a wall decoration for everyone to enjoy.

Roasted Pumpkin Seeds

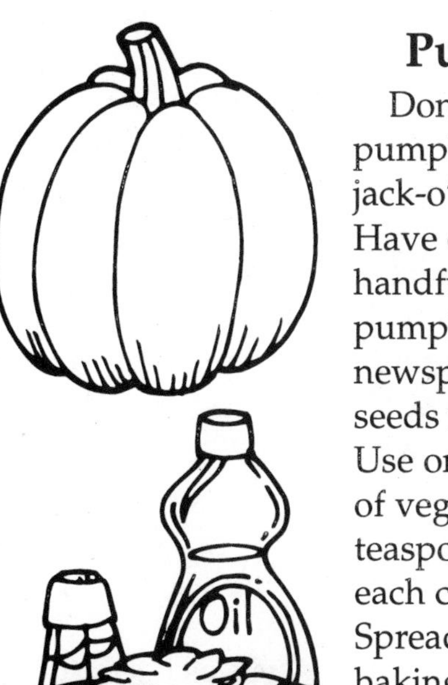

Don't throw away those pumpkin seeds from your jack-o'-lantern—roast them! Have each student take a handful or so out of the pumpkin. Then on a newspaper, separate the seeds from the string fibers. Use one tablespoon (15 ml) of vegetable oil and one teaspoon (5 ml) of salt for each cup of pumpkin seeds. Spread it all on the oiled baking sheet. Bake for about 45 minutes at 250° and let cool several minutes after they are removed from the oven.

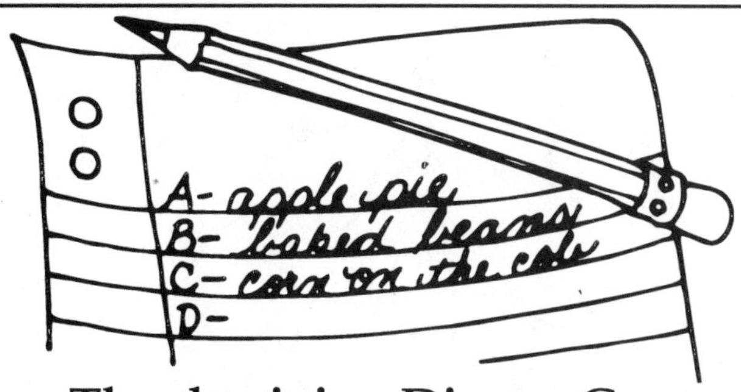

Thanksgiving Dinner Game

Assign each student a certain letter of the alphabet. The student must then think of a food for a Thanksgiving dinner that begins with that particular letter. Example:

A—apple pie
B—baked beans
C—corn on the cob

This could also work well as a written exercise: each student tries to find a certain food for every letter of the alphabet. If necessary, students can use reference books for additional help.

Making Turkey Tails

Here's a fall project to use all those gorgeous leaves you pressed in heavy books. This Thanksgiving turkey will put them to good use.

Separate pressed leaves into large, medium, and small sizes. Oak, maple, and similar-sized leaves would be considered large leaves. Aspen, beech, ash, elm, or cherry would be medium; and locust, chestnut, cottonwood, birch, or willow would be considered small. Judge your collection of leaves and sort them. Each category (large, medium, and small) should contain only one kind of leaf for each turkey.

First, use three to five large colorful leaves (all oak, all maple, and so on) and arrange in fan shape on a large piece of heavy paper. Glue down in an overlapping fashion with the stems all originating from one central point.

Second, select three to five medium leaves and glue down in the same fan shape over the first row of larger leaves.

Third, choose as many small leaves as needed to arrange a final row over the medium-sized middle row.

Make copies of the turkey's head and body for students to color or paint. Cut out and glue on top of the last row of small leaves. Your Thanksgiving turkey will be a great reminder of those vibrant autumn colors.

Thanksgiving Cookbook

Have your class create a Thanksgiving cookbook. Each student writes one recipe. The fun part of this project is that students make up their own recipes. (You may have to write or help younger children with their recipes.) It's much easier to have students write on 8" x 5" (20 x 13 cm) recipe cards. Students can illustrate their cards if they have enough space and then display them on your Thanksgiving Feast bulletin board.

Hints

- Be sure to explain what a recipe card should contain.
- Let students choose their favorite kinds of foods for their recipes. Talk about a balanced diet, good nutrition, and so on.
- Run off copies of the recipes and make a cookbook to send home to parents. They will enjoy it!

Decorative Thanksgiving Plate

Cut out a circle from orange posterboard and cover it with a paper doily. Trim the posterboard circle to match the doily. Glue a soft foam picnic plate to the center. Next, cut a circle of brown construction paper the same size as the picnic plate and glue it to the bottom of the plate. Leave edges of the construction paper unglued and fold up to form a ruffle. Glue ribbon along the inside edge of the ruffle as shown in the picture. Add pumpkins and leaves cut from construction paper. Write *We Give Thanks* on the plate and add gold glitter for extra sparkle.

Santa Door Decoration

This Christmas door decoration works great when used in conjunction with a map unit. Another fun activity can also be completed at the same time using a map of your city. Each student should have a copy of the map. Students then draw Santa's route to their houses (assuming Santa is coming from the north of town). For younger students, this map can be mailed along with letters to Santa.

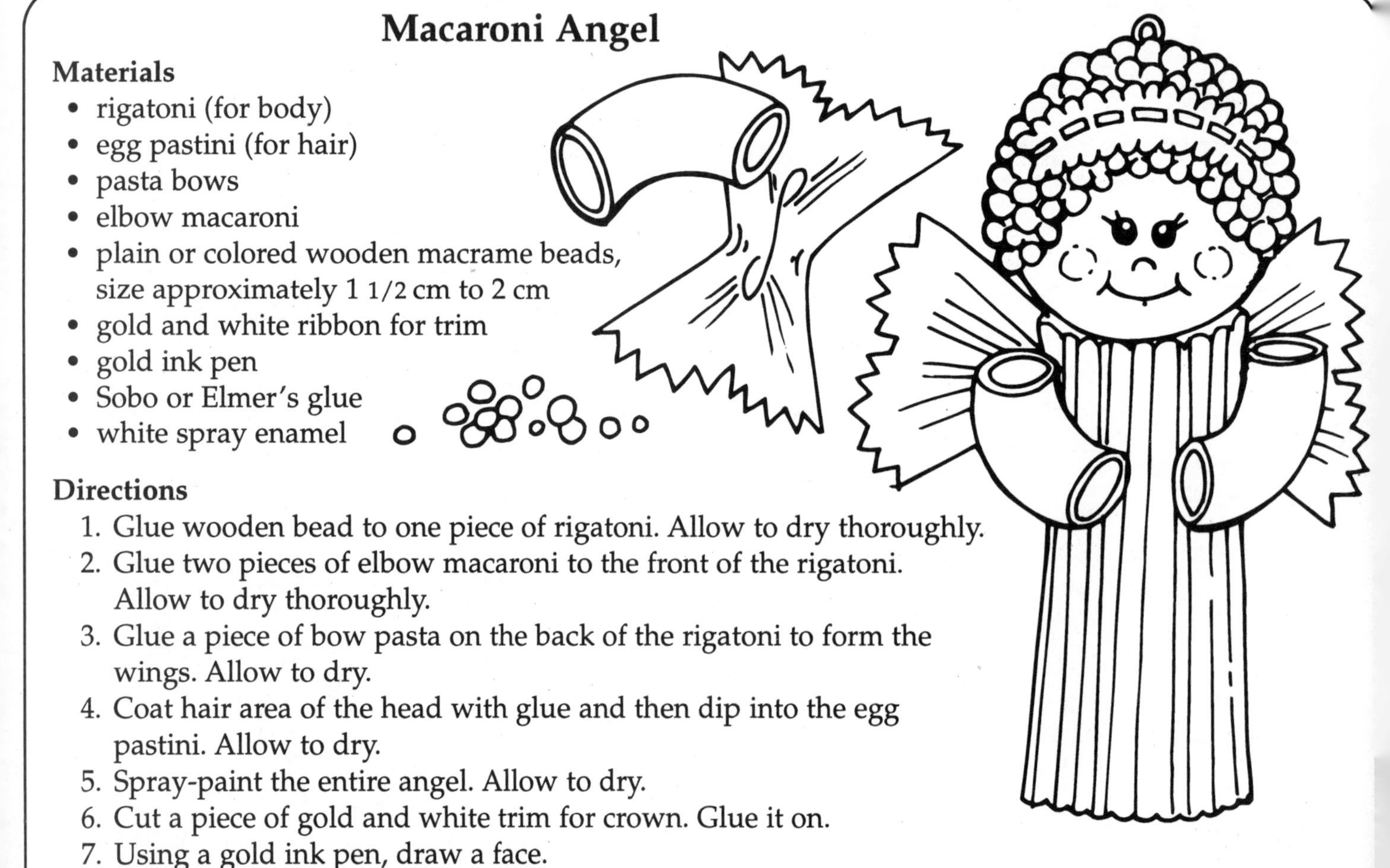

Macaroni Angel

Materials

- rigatoni (for body)
- egg pastini (for hair)
- pasta bows
- elbow macaroni
- plain or colored wooden macrame beads, size approximately 1 1/2 cm to 2 cm
- gold and white ribbon for trim
- gold ink pen
- Sobo or Elmer's glue
- white spray enamel

Directions

1. Glue wooden bead to one piece of rigatoni. Allow to dry thoroughly.
2. Glue two pieces of elbow macaroni to the front of the rigatoni. Allow to dry thoroughly.
3. Glue a piece of bow pasta on the back of the rigatoni to form the wings. Allow to dry.
4. Coat hair area of the head with glue and then dip into the egg pastini. Allow to dry.
5. Spray-paint the entire angel. Allow to dry.
6. Cut a piece of gold and white trim for crown. Glue it on.
7. Using a gold ink pen, draw a face.
8. Paste gold ribbon loop at the top if you wish to hang on the Christmas tree.

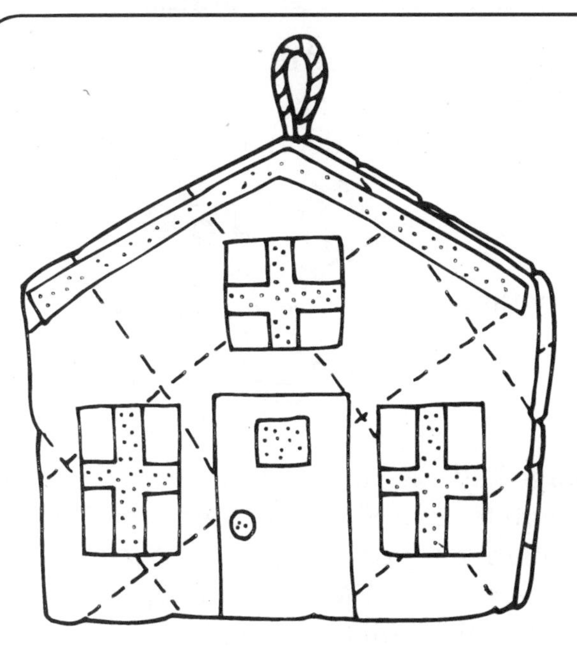

Christmas Tree House Ornaments

Cut out a cardboard pattern of a house. Trace the pattern of the house onto another piece of cardboard. Glue quilted cotton cloth cut from the same pattern onto both sides of your cardboard house. Cut out colorful felt windows and doors to glue onto both sides. Using white glue, cut out and glue felt strips along the edges of the roof on each side. Staple a yarn loop to the top of the house to hang on your tree.

A Christmas Tree Game

The boys compete against the girls in this game. Each student has a piece of paper to be decorated like a package tied with a ribbon. The student's name is printed on the front. On the opposite side of the package, draw a picture of a toy. Show each package and its toy to students and name its owner. Pin all of the packages onto the wall tree. Now boys compete against the girls, with alternate turns. They try to guess which toy is on the back of each package. Tell only the name on the package. Keep score to see if the boys or girls win.

Your Own Small Christmas Tree

Materials

- large thread spool
- small evergreen branch
- bits of ribbon, paper, or buttons for trim

Directions

Decorate the thread spool with bits of red and green ribbon, rickrack, or Christmas wrapping paper. Push an evergreen branch into the hole of the spool for the small tree. Decorate the tree with tiny paper chains, ribbons, bows, paper stars, buttons, or other small trim.

A Holiday Welcome

This do-it-yourself decoration is a nice holiday welcome for guests. It doesn't take long to make this doorknob decoration.

Materials
- red and green felt
- odds and ends of decorative trims
- glitter
- jingle bells

Directions
1. On paper, draw a large keyhole pattern. Be sure the keyhole is large enough to cover the area around your doorknob. Pin the pattern on green felt and cut it out with regular scissors or pinking shears. Make another paper keyhole pattern that is slightly smaller than the first. After you cut this pattern out of red felt, glue the smaller red keyhole onto the larger green keyhole.
2. Trim the decoration with braids or rickrack. Make small dots of glue and sprinkle with gold or silver glitter. Add a few jingle bells, ribbon, or holly.
3. Finally, fit the decoration over the doorknob. Find the center of the top of the keyhole. With sharp scissors, cut 1" (2.5 cm) slits from the center in eight directions. (See example.) Now the decoration is ready to slip over the doorknob for a holiday welcome.

Christmas Pie Tins

Materials
- disposable aluminum pie tins
- old Christmas cards
- rickrack
- glue
- glue-on picture hanger

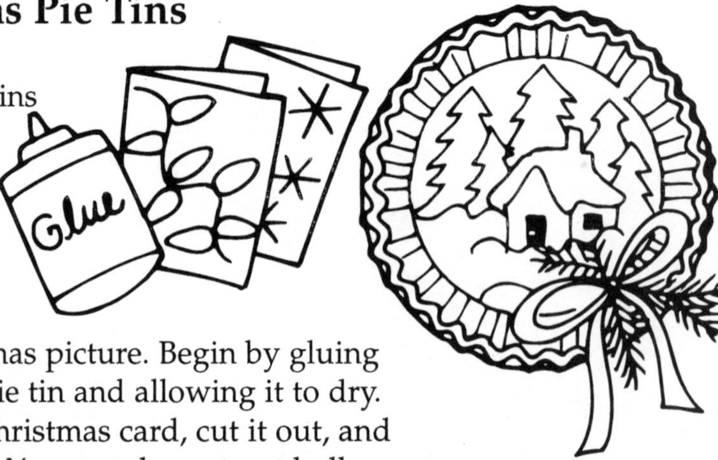

Directions
1. This simple craft makes a very pretty Christmas picture. Begin by gluing rickrack trim around the outside rim of the pie tin and allowing it to dry.
2. Choose a nice picture or scene from an old Christmas card, cut it out, and glue the picture onto the inside of the pie tin. You can also cut out holly leaves from the cards and glue them onto the rickrack border for a nice festive touch.
3. Ribbon or other decorative trims can also be added. Finally attach a glue-on picture hanger to the back of the pie tin, and it is ready to hang.

Bottle Cap Wreath

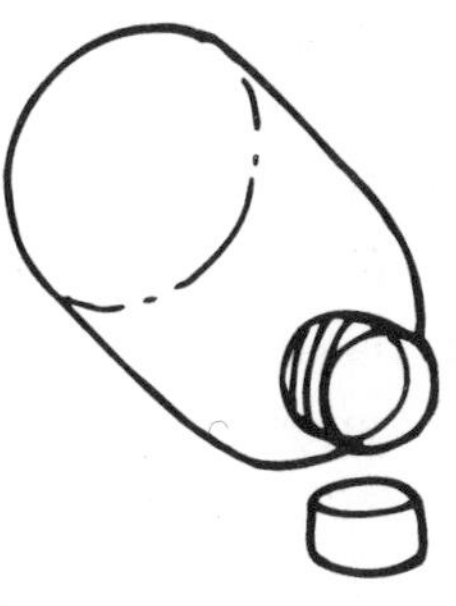

Materials
- caps from soda bottles
- fabric scraps
- 12" x 12" (30 x 30 cm) cardboard
- 12" x 12" (30 x 30 cm) green construction paper, fabric, or felt
- crêpe paper
- glue or glue gun

Directions
1. Twist-off soda bottle caps can be made into an interesting Christmas wreath. Start the wreath by placing a large dinner plate on the cardboard and tracing around it. Cut out this circle, making the cutting line a bit wavy. Cut out a small circle in the center, and you have a wreath shape. Cover the cardboard with green paper or fabric.
2. Now cut small circles from fabric. Each circle should have a 2 1/2" (6 cm) diameter. Glue the fabric circles over the bottle caps, stuffing the outer edges inside the cap. When all the caps are covered and the glue is dry, glue the caps open-side up onto your wreath base. You may need to add a dot of glue inside each cap to keep the fabric in place. Add a bright red crêpe-paper bow to the wreath, and it is ready to hang.

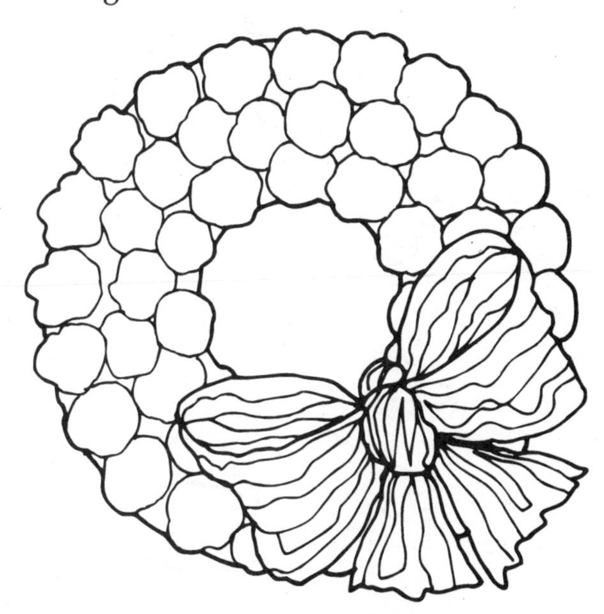

Christmas Card Holder

Materials
- cereal box
- construction paper
- cotton balls
- paper stars
- glue

Directions
1. Cut off the top of a cereal box so the front and back are about 6" (15 cm) high and the sides are about 4" (10 cm) high.
2. Cover the box with dark blue or black construction paper. Cut a circle from pink construction paper for a Santa face. Also cut out small circles for Santa's eyes, nose, and mouth and glue on the face in the proper places. From red construction paper, make a Santa hat and glue the hat on Santa's head.
3. Glue Santa's head onto the box. Use cotton balls to make Santa's beard and trim his hat. Glue the paper stars to the dark paper background. When Christmas cards start to arrive, they can be kept in this festive holder.

Winter Picnic

Tired of those long, indoor lunch hours due to subzero weather or storms? Try a winter picnic! Clear the center of the room and eat lunches there. For "extras," make Eskimo sandwiches, serve an ice-cream treat, bake white cupcakes covered with coconut, or serve real "snow cones" with syrup poured over them. Just eating lunch in the room is a big thrill.

How about asking each family to fix the student's lunch with all white food? White bread, milk, cauliflower, white cupcake, popcorn—see how imaginative a family can be.

Winter Scavenger Hunt

Learn more about winter and cold weather by planning an outdoor scavenger hunt with your class. Divide the class into pairs and give each pair a plastic bag. (You may group children by those with the same birthday month, those wearing red shirts, those who live in a white house, and so on.) Set a time limit and boundary lines on the school property. Challenge students to find one item in each category.

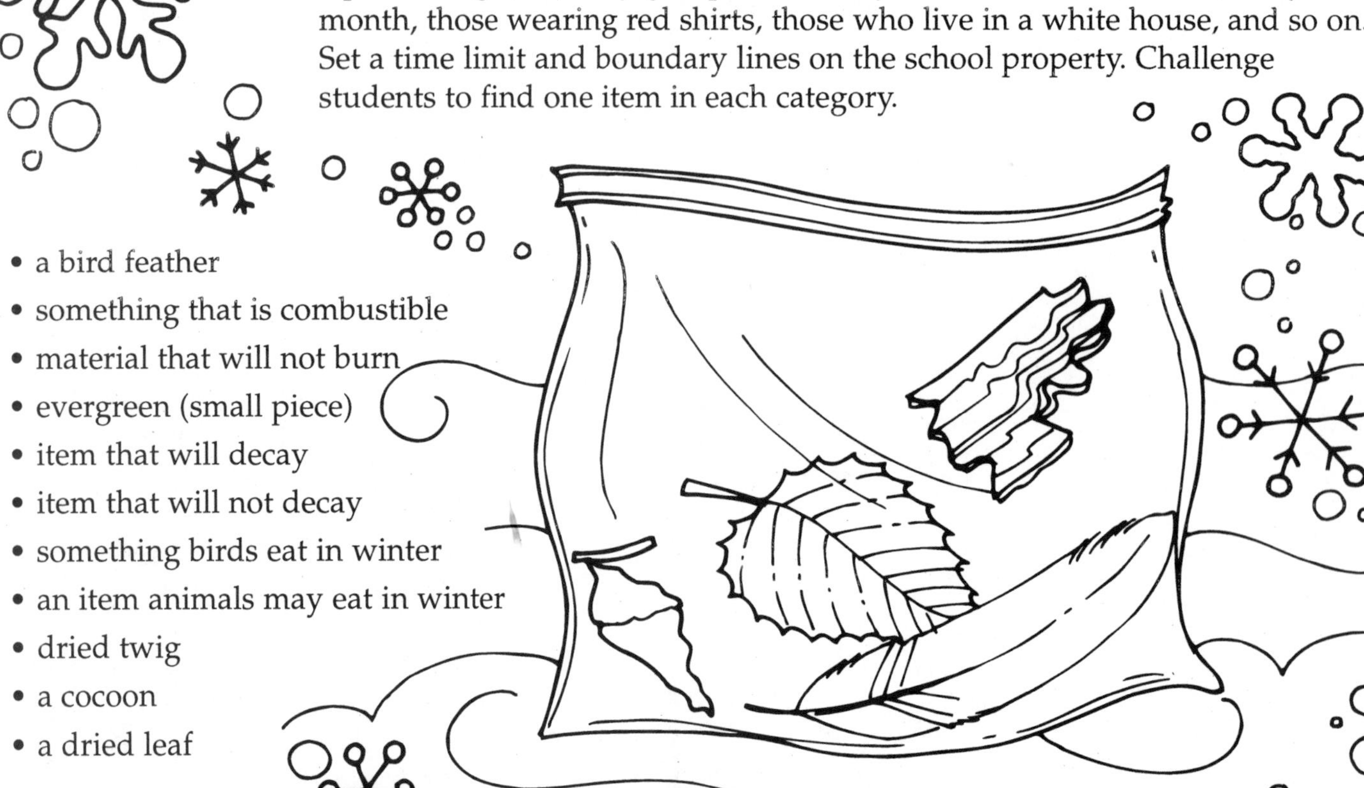

- a bird feather
- something that is combustible
- material that will not burn
- evergreen (small piece)
- item that will decay
- item that will not decay
- something birds eat in winter
- an item animals may eat in winter
- dried twig
- a cocoon
- a dried leaf

General

Teacher Tips

Fact-for-the-Day

Fact-for-the-Day is a small tidbit of interesting information that you can find in the newspaper, a book of world records, or any book of trivia. Write the information on sheets of paper or small posters.

Every morning, put out a new fact-for-the-day. Place it in a very visible location. Students should read it some time during the morning. During the afternoon, ask a question about the fact that requires only a "yes" or "no" answer. The answer should be written down and handed in to you. Quiz students a couple of times during the week to keep them on their toes and to require them to retain the information.

These facts can be laminated and used each year. A permanent clip or clothespin glued to a board or wall makes daily changing very easy.

Birthday Idea

Materials

- strips of paper in graduating lengths
- magic markers
- glue
- tacks
- glitter

The birthday child gets the shortest strip of paper. He or she writes his or her name on the strip. Classmates receive the other strips of paper. On the strip, students write their names and something about themselves. For example: Mary Smith likes to read. Tom Butler got an A in science; and so on. Each student then glues his or her strip on a large sheet of paper. The bottom strip should be the longest and the strips should gradually decrease in length as they move up the paper. When complete, you and your students have created a giant birthday cake for the birthday person to keep. You may wish to turn this idea into a permanent bulletin board area in your classroom. Just add paper candles!

Collecting Postmarks

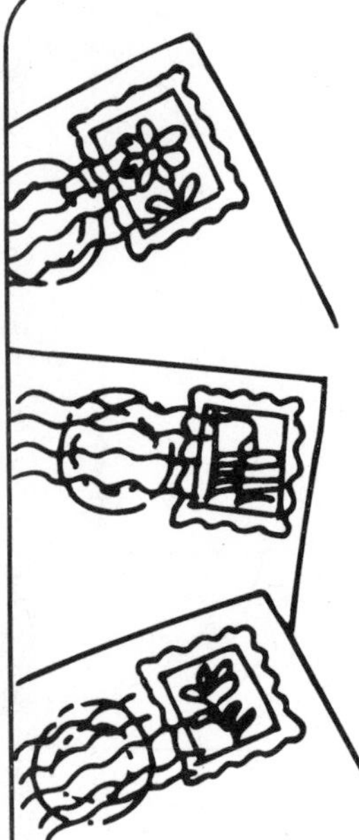

Begin your own collection of postmarks. You'll need writing paper, No. 10 business envelopes, postcards, and the proper postage for each card.

Have students write letters to the postmaster in towns of their choice, asking him or her to hand-cancel the postcard. Have them ask about how the towns got their names. The postmaster can write this information on the back of the postcard. Address the letter to the United States Post Office, with the town's name, state, and ZIP code. Write your address on the postcard for the reply.

Mail the letter, with the postcard inside. After a few weeks, you'll begin to receive your postmarks and replies.

Post 'em

Once the postcards start rolling in, post them on a bulletin board to share with the class. Add a U.S. map and mark the locations of the cities as you receive the replies. Since many of these towns are very small, you'll need a good atlas to find their exact locations.

Keep on Your Toes!

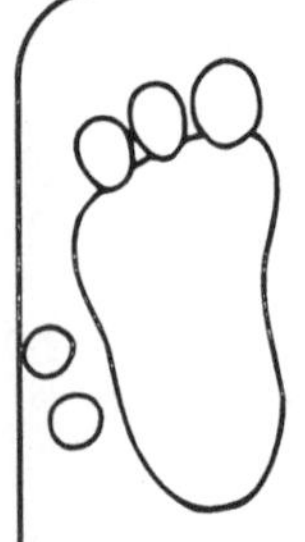

1. Divide the class into teams.
2. Each team is given two paper feet with 10 detachable toes. (This may also be drawn on the board.)
3. Ask each team member a review question alternating teams.
4. If a wrong answer is given, off comes a toe.
5. The team with the most toes remaining is the winner.

Feedback

How much do you talk in your classroom? Not enough? Too much? Try this activity several times during a week for various methods. Write down how much time you want to talk during a particular lesson and how much student talking you want. Then borrow a couple of stopwatches from the coach. Give a student a watch and ask him or her to run it while you are talking. Give another student the second watch and have it run when students are talking. Check your results with your predictions.

Feelin' Good Again

Sometimes a student is sick for a period of time or in the hospital. Have the class cut pieces of yellow paper to resemble potato chips. Each student writes his or her get-well wishes on a paper chip. These greetings are placed inside a decorated, empty Pringle's® can and are delivered to the sick student with the following instructions: "Take two a day until you are feeling chipper."

It's in the Bag

Save paper bags of various sizes and request students, parents, and colleagues to contribute some also. The wider the variety the better. When you get enough for three bags per student, distribute different brands/sizes and have students list as many different ways to use the bags as they can. Give examples such as book covers, lunch bags, gift wrap, shopping bags. The ideas must be different for each. For example, they cannot count a book cover for math and a book cover for English as separate ideas. Then make a chart or graph showing all the uses students came up with.

Have students make a list of any print on the bags, such as company name, recycled logo, colors or numbers used, pictures, slogans, or dimensions. Make a graph showing the percentage of bags with the symbol for recycled paper, how many were printed in Kentucky, how many were used by a certain store, and so on.

Then have students each decorate one of the bags (save the others) and use it to take home school projects. Another project would be to make greeting cards using stencils, paint, scraps of construction paper, yarn, stickers, old greeting cards, and so on. Also, Valentine's Day; National Be Kind to Animals Week; or Martin Luther King, Jr. Day are some of the special events you could commemorate by decorating bags.

Tic-Tac-Know

Directions

1. Divide the class into two teams—TIC and TAC.
2. The teacher is KNOW.
3. Ask review questions to each team member, alternating teams.
4. If the team member has answered correctly, he or she places a marker anywhere on the grid.
5. If the student doesn't answer correctly, the other team gets a chance.
6. If neither team member knows the answer, then the teacher responds and places a KNOW marker on the grid.
7. The first team to get three markers in a row wins the game.

Boosting Self-Esteem With Biographies

When studying biographies, go one step further and have students write biographies about their classmates. Every Friday, draw one student's name to be the "special person" for the following week. This student will also write his or her own life story as an autobiography.

The "special person" should stand in front of the room to be interviewed by the teacher. Some sample questions can be found here, but be sure to include some of your own.

- Have you gone to this school since kindergarten, or have you gone to other schools? Tell us about it.
- What is your favorite color? food? school subject? TV program? book?
- Do you have brothers or sisters? Tell about them.
- Do you ride the bus to school?
- What do you like to do in your spare time?

Students can then ask the special student anything they want to know about pets and so on. Ask students to write at least a one-page biography using the information given in the interview and anything else he or she can remember about the student. Make it clear that only good things should be written about each other.

The interview from the teacher and the attention from peers can be a real ego boost. The authors also feel very proud of their work. Make a cover for the biographies and send them home for the families to read.

Classroom Balloons

Fill a wastebasket or two with dime-store balloons, and the stage is set for some party-style learning! Make colored chalk balloons on the board and write in these questions:

1. What color is the balloon with the greatest circumference?
2. What color is the balloon with the smallest circumference?
3. Measure the circumference of three balloons. What is the sum of the circumferences of the three?
4. What is the difference between the smallest and greatest circumference?
5. How many balloons would fit in our wastebasket? The volume of the wastebasket is ___ balloons.

The balloons can be used for many learning activities. Before you blow up the balloons, place a story starter in each one. Write the story starter on a small piece of paper. Before going to recess, each student selects a balloon and takes it outside to break. Students save the story starters and, when recess is over, return to the classroom and begin work on the stories.

Use a marker to write one number on each balloon. Students can find the total of all the balloons and create as many math sentences as possible using the numerals on the balloons. What is the total of all red balloons? How much more is the total of the yellow balloons than the total of the blue balloons?

Calendar Cut-Ups

Calendars provide an abundant and inexpensive source of teacher-made classroom aids. New calendars, of course, can be used to keep track of the days, months, birthdays, special classroom activities, and assignments. Weather symbols can be added daily and later used to chart or graph weather patterns.

Once the calendar is outdated, it can be even more valuable as a classroom aid. With construction paper, tagboard, clear contact paper, and a little ingenuity, many useful teaching tools can be made.

Cut apart the numbered squares from a calendar page, mount on tagboard, and laminate. These can be used to sequence the numbers from 1 to 31. For self-checking, mount and laminate an intact calendar page to be used to check against. For children who do not yet know their numbers, they might simply match the cut-apart squares to the complete page.

Tiny flashcards can be made by cutting and mounting the names of the days of the week and the names of the months. These can be used for sequencing, writing practice, and matching activities, as well as flashcards.

Many calendars have colorful pictures that can also be mounted and laminated for use in a variety of ways. They might be useful in stimulating discussions, language-experience stories, or as motivators for creative writing. They also make colorful additions to classroom bulletin boards and classroom walls.

Staple a calendar page to one side of an open file folder. Type a list of questions that can be answered by referring to that page and staple it to the other side of the folder. Ask questions such as:

- How many Sundays are in the month?
- On what day of the week does the fifteenth fall?
- On what day does the month start?
- What month comes before this one?
- How many days are in the month?
- What is the date of the third Tuesday?

Put an answer key on the back of the folder and laminate. Make a similar folder with two small calendar pages inside. Ask comparative questions such as "Which month has more days?" "In which month does the twelfth fall on a Saturday?"

Have students use an almanac or encyclopedia to locate famous (and infamous) dates in history. Let them enter the events on the proper dates on a calendar. Encourage them to fill in as many dates as possible. Then challenge other students to pick a date and research the happening to write a report or news article explaining the significance of the occurrence. Use famous birthdays, inventions (bubblegum, balloons, computers, and so on), great battles, historical events, and so on.

General

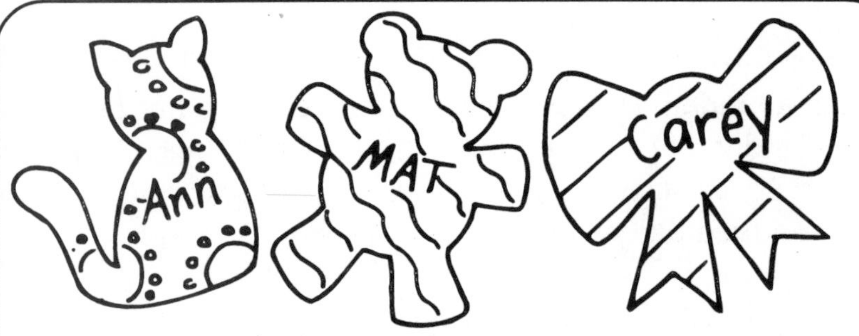

Stencils for Cats, Bears, and More

If your school has a machine that cuts stencils, just cut wallpaper to size and cut the desired shape. These are good for accenting a bulletin board that has a matching wallpaper border. The stencils can be used for nametags students can wear on the first day of school, to tape on the student's desk, to post around the room as indicators of how to find certain objects, and on posters.

Note Paper or Christmas Cards

Wallpaper, cut to the size of prepurchased envelopes, makes a personalized gift or card for each student. The back needs to be checked to find areas without printing. Otherwise, stencils cut from wallpaper can be glued to plain paper for stationery or note cards.

Wrapping Paper

If a gift is small enough, wallpaper can be folded and used for wrapping. Stencils can be glued to paper sacks and used as gift bags for putting students' Mother's Day, Christmas, or other gifts inside.

Covers for Student Reports

To get students in the habit of making their reports look special, or as a reward for doing an outstanding job, give students wallpaper to add "class" to their finished reports. Titles need to be written with dark-colored permanent markers or printed on an attached label.

Book Covers for Child-Made Books

Wallpaper can be cut to the size of your book and stapled to the outside. Paper that has been rejected by the copy machine makes good inserts. For more substantial books, glue the wallpaper on tagboard, stitch your pages together, and glue the two outside pages to the tagboard.

Pockets for Learning Centers

Plain folders don't get much of a response and it takes a long time to color pictures to use on them. Wallpaper may be just what you need to entice your learners to look inside an activity pocket.

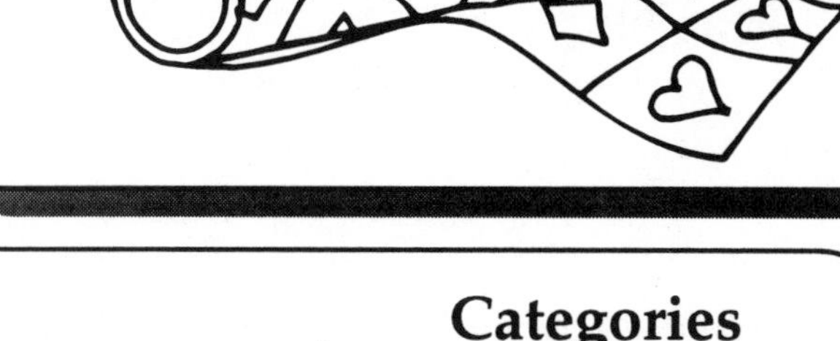

Mystery Animal Day

Delight students with a Mystery Animal Day. First, label five or six colorful folders with the words *Mystery Packet.* In each folder, put an information sheet or magazine article about a different animal. Divide your class into teams of about four or five students, and ask them to quietly read the information about their mystery animals. Next, have the team write five clues about the identity of its animal. Set an appropriate time limit for this activity. Have sharing time for each group to present its clues to the class, then have the audience try to guess the animal's identity.

Recycle your mystery packets again! Have more "mystery" days using other subjects, such as plants, space, and inventions.

Categories

Barnyard Animals
COW
PIG
CHICKEN
LAMB
GOAT

Players choose a category such as foreign countries, cars, games, trees, barnyard animals, TV shows, musical instruments, nursery rhymes, holidays, fruits, rocks, and so on. Use simple categories for younger students and more difficult categories for older students. Each player names something within the category. When a player cannot think of an item in the category, the player is out. The last player left is the winner.

Envelopes for Storing Supplies

Even teachers can find folders monotonous and difficult to tell apart. A unique wallpaper design might be just the trick for finding the supplies you need. Use postal tape to turn your paper folders into envelopes for the most permanent solution.

Whatchamacallit

For this relay, students must race to the opposite end of the room, choose a book from a pile of books at the head of each team, recite the call letters/numbers, and then return to the team line. The first team to complete the relay wins.

From the Earth to the Moon

This game may be played two ways. First, cut out a construction-paper Earth, moon, and rocket. Position the Earth and moon on a bulletin board or chalkboard. Have students solve math problems or answer other questions to blast off, travel through space, then safely land on the moon. Each student who answers correctly comes up and moves the rocket closer to the moon. In another version, each student receives a printed sheet showing the Earth and moon and a numbered trajectory between them. The number in the trajectory corresponds to the number of questions in a true/false quiz about the moon. After students take the quiz, discuss the answers in class. For every correct answer, students circle another number in the trajectory. Whoever gets 100 percent has reached the moon.

The Terrific Taste Test

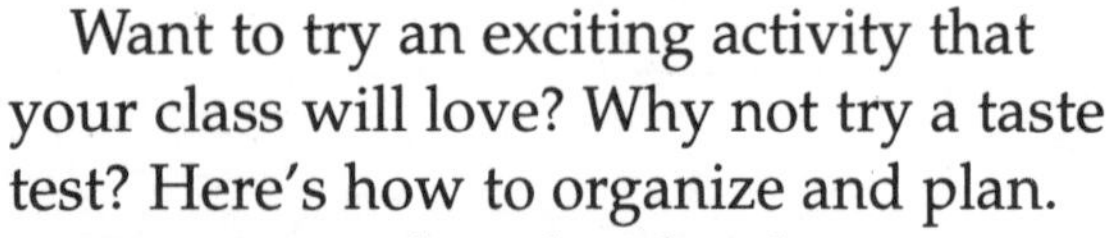

Want to try an exciting activity that your class will love? Why not try a taste test? Here's how to organize and plan.

Have your class decide what two products to use in your taste test. Some good examples are two different brands of fruit punch, granola bars, yogurt, crackers, or cookies.

The next step is to have students design a survey sheet to be filled out by those participating in the taste test. Be sure to include a space for students to comment on why they preferred certain products.

Then have students decorate the area for the taste test with colorful posters and signs. You may want them to make invitations to invite other classes to participate. They should also make signs to label the two products being tested.

Finally, the big day for the taste test has arrived! Have students set up several tables with the foods to be tested. As the participants meet in the area, have a host hand out the survey forms and direct them to one of the tables.

Have a team of students responsible for tallying the results and writing a report on your survey. If your school has a newspaper, you may want to have students write an article for it.

To further extend this activity, have students create an advertising campaign for one of the products in the taste test. This can include a catchy ad for a magazine complete with artwork and a radio or television commercial. Students can work individually or in teams.

Book Jackets

Choose several books with durable jackets which can easily be removed. Have teams race to the book, take the jacket off, and give the jacket to the team member at the start of the line. The next student must run down and put the jacket back on. The team that finishes first wins.

Order Up Some Books

Pile several books at the head of each team. Have each student skip down to other end of the room, place the books in ABC order, have them checked by a referee, and then return with the books, giving them to the next team member, who completes the same activity. Play continues until one team finishes first.

Mark It

Give each team captain a sturdy bookmark. Each student on the team must hop down to the book, lay the bookmark on a page designated by the referee, close the book, and then hop back. The next student hops down, moves the bookmark to a particular place, and hops back. Play continues until you have a winning team.

Title It

Place a large sheet of paper or chalkboard at the opposite end of the room for each team. Ask students to correctly write the title of a book, using capital letters and proper punctuation. As children cross the room to complete the activity, observe their response and then dictate new titles for students who follow. The team that finishes first wins.

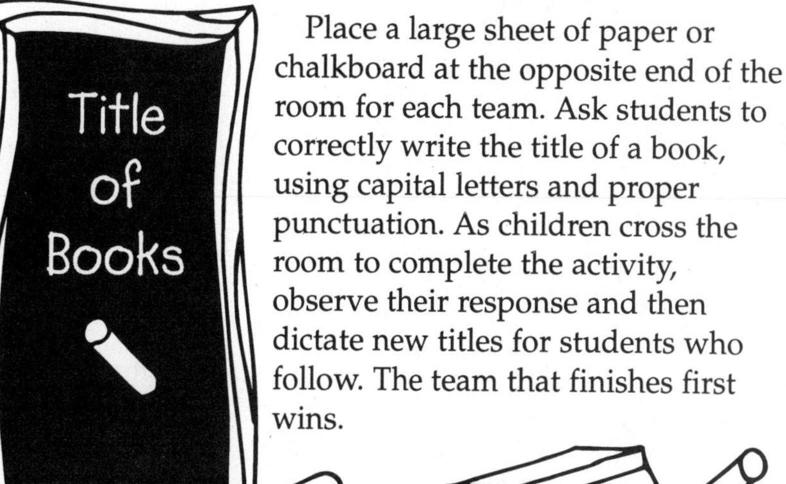

Book Sale

Have your math students open a bookstore. Send a flyer to fellow teachers in your building asking for old books or salespersons' copies. Students could also be asked to bring books from home. Decide on a price for the books, such as 5¢ each. Students are clerks and also plan the advertising campaign. Discuss how to spend the proceeds. What would you like to buy for your classroom? What would all students enjoy and be able to use? What would be the best price you could find?

The Imaginary Class

Many times, when students want to read stories aloud to someone, other students do not really want to listen. Have each student draw an 18" picture of an imaginary student who likes to listen to stories. Put these on the wall in a secluded corner of the room. When a student wants to read a story to the imaginary class, have him or her sit in the "teacher's" chair and read aloud with good expression. Then have the student fill out a short book report form. Students are extremely motivated to read, and each wants a chance to be the "teacher" for the imaginary class. A tape recorder should be placed in this area so that you can listen to students at a later time.

Basketball Review Game

Duplicate about 30 of the basketballs above on brown paper. On the back of each basketball, write a review question from any unit. Some basketballs should have *foul, free throw,* or *traveling* written on the back. *Free throw* automatically equals 1 point. *Foul or Traveling* means no questions asked and no points given. All other questions equal 2 points. Divide the class into two teams. Flip a coin to decide which team goes first. To play the game, start with all basketballs (about 30) numbered and arranged on the chalkboard (taped) to form one large ball. Students then pick their questions by simpy calling out numbers. If one team doesn't know an answer, the opponents can "steal the ball" and answer the question.

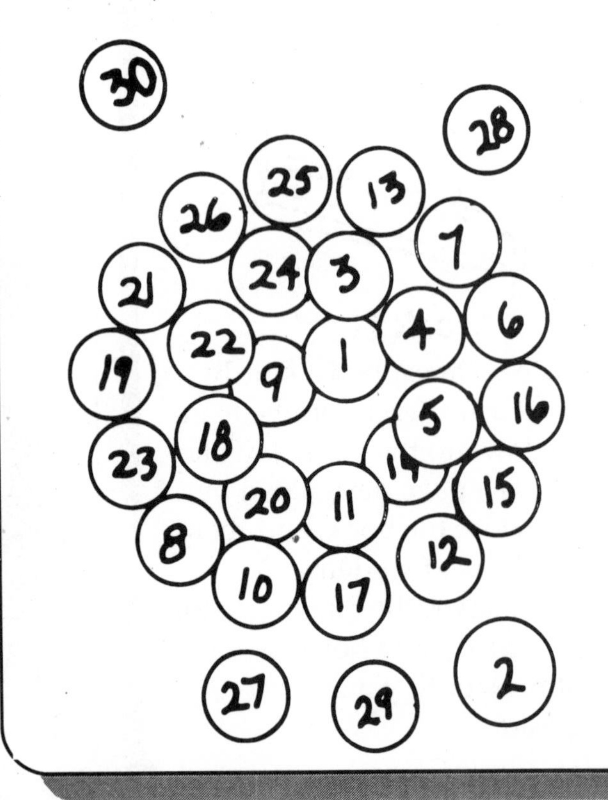